Elaine Segal

Making Contact

A TIME TO SPEAK

NONVERBAL COMMUNICATION

MOVIES: Conversations with Peter Bogdanovich

ELECTRIC MEDIA

VISUAL PERSUASION

PRINT MEDIA

 Consultant: Louis Forsdale, Teachers College, Columbia University

*A program developed for Harcourt Brace Jovanovich by Paul McCluskey,
with the assistance of Francine Weinberg, Fannie Safier, and Deborah Hyman.*

A TIME TO SPEAK

Howard Stein

Special Contributors
Dustin Hoffman
Kurt Vonnegut, Jr.

Harcourt Brace Jovanovich, Inc.
New York Chicago San Francisco Atlanta Dallas

Howard Stein is Associate Dean of the Yale School of Drama and an adjunct professor of playwriting. He has also taught at the University of Iowa, the University of New Hampshire, and Northeastern University. Dr. Stein is a five-time winner of the Samuel French award for excellence in the teaching of playwriting.

ACKNOWLEDGMENTS: For permission to reprint copyrighted material grateful acknowledgment is made to the following:

Norma Millay Ellis: "Departure" from *Collected Poems* by Edna St. Vincent Millay, copyright 1923, 1951 by Edna St. Vincent Millay and Norma Millay Ellis. Published by Harper & Row.

Holt, Rinehart and Winston, Inc., Jonathan Cape Limited, and the Estate of Robert Frost: "Home Burial" from *The Poetry of Robert Frost* edited by Edward Connery Lathem, copyright 1930, 1939, © 1969 by Holt, Rinehart and Winston; copyright © 1958 by Robert Frost; copyright © 1967 by Lesley Frost Ballantine.

Macmillan Publishing Co., Inc., A. P. Watt & Son, the Macmillan Co. of London & Basingstoke, the Macmillan Co. of Canada Ltd., and Mr. M. B. Yeats: "The Song of Wandering Aengus" from *The Collected Poems of William Butler Yeats,* copyright 1906 by Macmillan Publishing Co., Inc.; renewed 1934 by William Butler Yeats.

The New York Times Company: Excerpts from a debate between Germaine Greer and William F. Buckley, Jr., from an article entitled "Oh, The Things They're Debating at Cambridge" from *The New York Times,* February 24, 1973, © 1973 by The New York Times Company.

Random House, Inc.: From *When She Was Good* by Philip Roth, copyright © 1967 by Philip Roth. "The New South" from *Major Campaign Speeches of Adlai Stevenson 1952.*

Flora Roberts, Inc., as Agent for Alice Childress: String by Alice Childress, © copyright, 1971, by Alice Childress. CAUTION: The amateur production rights of *String* are controlled exclusively by the Dramatists Play Service, Inc., 440 Park Avenue South, New York, N.Y. 10016. No amateur performance of the play may be given without obtaining advance written permission from the Dramatists Play Service, Inc. All inquiries concerning rights (other than the amateur rights) should be addressed to the author's agent, Flora Roberts, Inc., 116 East 59 Street, New York, N.Y. 10022.

Russell & Volkening, Inc., as Agents for the Author: Excerpt from "The Wrecker" from *Seize the Day* by Saul Bellow, copyright © 1954 by Saul Bellow.

Copyright © 1974 by Harcourt Brace Jovanovich, Inc.

All rights reserved. No part of this publication may be reproduced or transmitted in any form or by any means, electronic or mechanical, including photocopy, recording, or any information storage and retrieval system, without permission in writing from the publisher.

Printed in the United States of America

ISBN 0-15-318730-1

contents

A TIME TO KEEP SILENCE   2
The meanings of the phrase *shut up*. Being locked up inside yourself. The value of words and the limits of words. The hesitancies people feel about talking.

THE YOU NOBODY KNOWS   7
Examining your motives in everyday actions. How emotions affect speech. The individuality of voices and of people. Communication breakdown. The voice's power to communicate more than content. The elements of spoken communication.

SPEAK WHEN SPOKEN TO   18
The value of listening. The difficulties of listening and being listened to. The frustrations of not being listened to. Knowing the person you're talking to. The difference between communication and agreement.

MAKING CONTACT with Kurt Vonnegut, Jr.   29
A conversation in which the author of *Slaughterhouse-Five* and other major works discusses dialogue in plays and novels, the charm of words, the values of the printed word and the spoken word, the communication styles of different generations.

SAY IT WITH SPECIFICS   42
The importance of research, evidence, and specifics in communication. Curiosity and questioning.

SPEAK FOR YOURSELF   50
First activities in public speaking. Asking questions. Constructing a speech: beginnings, middles, and ends. A sample speech.

LOOK AT IT MY WAY 61
The place of persuasion in daily life. The conventions of persuasion. Logic versus emotion in persuasion.

LOOK AT IT HIS WAY 69
Analysis of the rhetorical devices used in a presidential campaign speech delivered by Adlai Stevenson in Richmond, Virginia.

LET'S AGREE TO DISAGREE 83
Informal varieties of disagreement: discussion, arguing, bickering. Formal discussion: committee discussions, panels, forums, symposiums, debate. A model debate between Germaine Greer and William F. Buckley, Jr., on the Women's Liberation Movement.

SAY IT WITH FEELING 97
Oral interpretation of prose and poetry: passages from conversations with Kurt Vonnegut, Jr., and Dustin Hoffman, and poems by William Butler Yeats, William Blake, Edna St. Vincent Millay, and Robert Frost

MAKING CONTACT with Dustin Hoffman 113
A conversation in which the actor discusses his preparation for stage and screen roles, building characters, and the place of voice and speech patterns in character portrayal.

PUT ON ANOTHER FACE 126
Basic introduction to acting. Pretending and imitating. The value of improvisation. Finding clues for character interpretation.

THE PLAY'S THE THING 135
Alice Childress's one-act play "String" with suggestions for adaptation.

THERE IS NO CONCLUSION 158
A reminder about questioning, seeking information and specifics, respecting individuality, and speaking intelligently from knowledge.

A TIME TO SPEAK

Silence is golden.

A TIME TO KEEP SILENCE

The title of your book comes from the biblical writings of a man who called himself the Preacher. He is better known as Ecclesiastes, and you probably are familiar with this passage, or have heard it set to music by Pete Seeger:

> To everything there is a season, and a time to every purpose under the heaven.
> A time to be born, and a time to die; a time to plant, and a time to pluck up that which is planted;
> A time to kill, and a time to heal; a time to break down, and a time to build up;
> A time to weep, and a time to laugh; a time to mourn, and a time to dance;
> A time to cast away stones, and a time to gather stones together; a time to embrace, and a time to refrain from embracing;
> A time to get, and a time to lose; a time to keep, and a time to cast away;
> A time to rend, and a time to sew; a time to keep silence, and a time to speak;
> A time to love, and a time to hate; a time of war, and a time of peace.

Ecclesiastes tells us there is a time for everything. And notice that he includes a time to keep silence. You might consider that to be the other half of the title of your book. What do you expect from a book that begins by suggesting that there is a time to keep silence and a time to speak? Would you have preferred a book called *Shut Up and Start*

A word spoken is past recalling.

Talking? That's not entirely unlike what Ecclesiastes says, is it? And that's what I'm suggesting to you as you begin to use this book. I've given your book a title that describes only half of the things I would like you to do as you use it.

Of course, it is discourteous and unmannerly to tell someone to shut up, and I don't want to be discourteous to you. Certainly, it will not help me to accomplish my objective — which is to get you to read this book seriously — if I offend you before you begin. That's why I'm not really telling you to shut up. Actually, I am telling you just the opposite. But think about *shut up* for a moment. What do you associate those words with? With someone telling you to be quiet? With someone shouting for silence? Some years ago, a very funny woman on television named Molly Goldberg used to say to her children, "Let me hear silence!" Does *shut up* mean someone telling you that you talk too much? Or someone telling you that you should stop talking nonsense? Would you also consider it to mean that a speaker can be inhibited or "shut up" within himself? Or not very free to express herself? I have considered all these possibilities, and some of them are more appropriate for my purposes than others. For instance, I think you should be aware of the nonsense you can speak and therefore try talking some sense. I believe that many of you should think before you speak — not all the time, but on more occasions than you do. I also think that many of you may feel shut up within yourselves, so much so that you are not sure what you would like to say or express. Obviously, I can be wrong in my assumptions. If I am, you and your fellow students and your teacher can decide in my absence.

This book is about talking and listening. That's why the first thing I would like you to do, after you discuss the title and my assumptions, is to communicate with somebody in your class for one minute *without saying a word*. How far can you get with that communication? The subject of your silent conversation can be your latest crush, your last class, the next game, last night, or your most recent purchase.

Did you succeed in getting across to your classmate what you wanted to say? How well did you communicate? Would using words to communicate have been more convenient, or perhaps even essential?

Would you have preferred to use words? Why, or why not? What have you discovered about the value, as well as the limits, of words? Words can only do certain things. They can harm as well as help. Shakespeare has Cleopatra describe Caesar to her friends by saying, "He words me, girls, he words me." What do you think Shakespeare meant by that statement?

No one thinks that words are perfect. But we all recognize that words can do a job for us. Hammers don't make very good saws, but for some tasks, such as knocking in nails, they can do the job well enough. Words can't tell you *exactly* how milk tastes, how love feels, how a nightmare left you trembling, what death seems like to you, or what new clothes do to your confidence. They admittedly cannot tell the whole truth about your most complex, secret, and deepest feelings or thoughts. But words can tell you *something* about all these aspects of your life, and they can be used to communicate expressions of much of your private world: personal feelings, pleasure, pain—so many things. For all these purposes, you need to know how to use words, especially for your own personal satisfaction.

Let me show you how badly I can talk. While I was writing this book, I taped a conversation with Kurt Vonnegut, Jr., for you to read. Listen to how poorly I talked to him at that time:

> For example, that the monologue even of a hero in that play, which seemed to me to be flowing with so much now freedom, gusto, then some of the dialogue, I remember feeling that memory. And also the marvelous . . . there are some individual characters . . . that Hungarian who had an extensive speech. But I also recall in that play that when the people, when there was a confrontation between the returning hero and his wife, and the returning hero and his son.

How's that for gibberish? When I heard the tape, I was embarrassed, and at this very moment you may wonder how you can expect to learn anything about talking and speech from a man who talks as I did then! (When you read the conversation later, you'll find that it makes more sense—because words on tape can be taken back and polished up a bit.) I offer that excerpt from my conversation precisely to show you that talking is not easy for anyone, not even for someone who's been doing it in front of students for over twenty years. Have you ever taped yourself talking and then been shocked at what you sounded like? I certainly have, and I was humiliated. However, I will try speaking to you with considerably more clarity than when I talked with Kurt Vonnegut, Jr.

There are no cure-alls or easy methods to learn to speak well or to speak clearly. Some of us learn to use words with more skill than others, and linguists, teachers, and parents still wonder why. This book doesn't intend to be any sort of remedy for the disease of poor speech. What it hopes to do is to help you become more conscious of what you are saying, and to give you some hints that may help you to be more articulate. Language usage is a great mystery. And the mystery lies dormant inside each one of us. For that reason, I encourage you to begin with yourself before you worry about the listeners to whom your communication is directed.

One word of digression may interest you here. In talking to my students about the value and beauty of history, I once made the point (before the days of Women's Lib) that history is *His Story,* the story of man, and studying it should be an exciting pursuit for anyone interested in the story of the human race. When I returned to my office a few hours after my lecture, I found a note left on my desk by one of my students:

> Dear Mr. Stein:
> History may be His Story, but mystery is My Story.

That student was smart. Every person is a mystery, and it is the unlocking of the mystery through all sorts of experiences and education that is essential to a meaningful and satisfying life.

There are really two kinds of speakers in the world: the first can describe a trip around the world and bore you completely, while the second can tell you about a visit to the neighborhood grocery store and make you thrill and vibrate.

I hope by the time you finish this book you will have unlocked your voice and found ways of expressing your feelings, thoughts, and fantasies. If that happens, I will consider the book to be a success.

At the back of this book, you will find a record I asked to make. I wanted a chance to talk as directly as I could to you. I hope you'll listen to what I have to say on the record as well as to what I have to say to you in your book. As I tell you on the record, if I could be in the classroom with you, we could have a conversation, and that would be nice. But I can't be there, so I'll try to speak as directly and clearly to you as I can. And I'd like you to speak to me — or write to me — if anything I have to say intrigues you.

To thine own self be true.

Getting to know yourself is a lifetime job. If you don't believe me, ask your parents. It takes a lifetime to learn how to live. But even at this stage of your life, you know something about yourself. You know that you have been courageous and that you have been cowardly, that you have been truthful and that you have told lies, that you have been kind and that you have been cruel, that you have been good and that you have been bad, that you have been right and that you have been wrong. The list is endless.

THE YOU NOBODY KNOWS

Perhaps you can recall particular times in your life that would illustrate the contradictions I have suggested. Perhaps you can add to that list of contradictions. These examples from your life should give you some insight into who you are, not what you would like to be or should have been. Instead, they will tell you what you have done and what you have said during certain moments of your life. They will tell you how you expressed certain feelings of the moment either in word or deed—expressions which reflected something of your mystery. They will not tell the whole story by any means. In fact, they will tell precious little. But they do reveal actual expressions of your character.

When you say you *know* somebody, what is it that you know? Do you believe that you really know anyone? Do you know some people better than others? Your mother? Father? Sister? Brother? Teacher? Friend? What do you really know when you think about these people? I suspect that you know something of their feelings. You know what situations turn them on or turn them off. You can predict what will get to them

Speech is a mirror of the soul.

and what won't affect them. That power of prediction comes from your having been exposed to these people in a number of past situations, and their reactions have registered with you. My children know that I am an easy touch when I am in a good mood. If they want an extra dollar, they will preface their request with, "Are you in a good mood today?" Chances are that you, like my children, are more conscious of other members of your family than you are of yourself. But if you are going to improve your speech or your ability to talk well, you are going to have to begin by being more conscious of who you are and what you feel.

Most people will tell you, as Kurt Vonnegut, Jr., tells you in his conversation later in this book, that you will speak well about something you feel strongly about. If you can speak well about something you feel strongly about, the task before you is to discover what you really know. Or, as Robert Frost would say, to know what you already know. The problem is precisely that: you must get to know what it is you know. It isn't a simple thing to do at all. We disguise much that we know from ourselves, particularly things about ourselves.

You are your fingerprints. In Washington there are recorded stacks of files that identify many of the citizens of this nation. That identification is in the form of fingerprints, for it is said that no two people have the same prints. Such a thought may be both pleasing and displeasing. It is pleasing to know that our individuality is so special and unique that there is no one in the world like any of us. On the other hand, the small differences in fingerprints remind us of larger differences that may cause us problems in communicating and living together.

The photograph on the opposite page shows a picture of a word being spoken. The pattern of wavy lines corresponds to different pitches of sound that were recorded by an electronic instrument called a *sound spectrograph*. Just as a camera can capture every detail of your features on light-sensitive film, so a sound spectrograph can record the individual characteristics of your voice.

The photograph is known as a *voiceprint* or *spectrogram*. Like the fingerprints that are unique to each of us, no two voiceprints are exactly alike. And that is hardly surprising when you consider all the factors that go into shaping a voice. Your voice is partly the result of

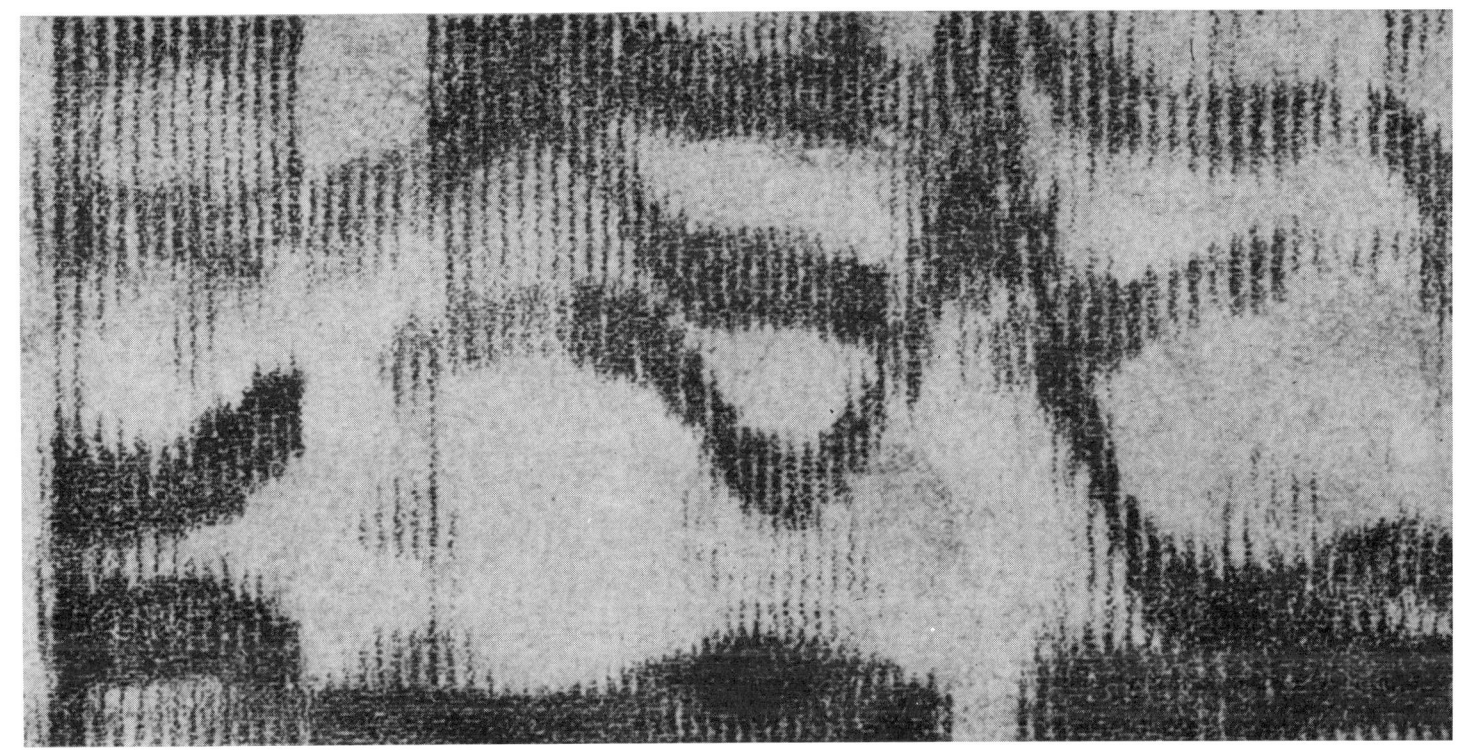

heredity. Length of vocal cords in part determines whether your voice is tenor, baritone, bass, soprano, or alto. And the quality of your voice—its resonance, huskiness, nasality—will be decided by physiological factors as well. But the patterns of your speech, the mannerisms and shadings that are special to you alone, are acquired throughout life and differ in varying degrees from one person to another.

Maybe you've seen a picture, now part of another time in communications, of a dog listening to a recording of his master's voice. The picture illustrates a phenomenon that is not uncommon. We have little difficulty recognizing a familiar voice on the telephone or when we answer the door or when a friend shouts to us from a distance. Even though millions of us have grown up in the same part of the country, have gone to similar schools and had the same teachers, have watched the same TV programs and films—despite all these factors which tend to make our language uniform, each of us still maintains an individual voice, an individual way of speaking that identifies each of us personally.

Of course, none of us ever hears the voice that others hear when we speak. We carry around an image or idea of the way we think we sound. When you hear yourself on tape for the first time, you're often surprised because the voice you hear is not the voice you think belongs to you. Sometimes you may not even recognize your own voice, although the words may seem familiar enough. The voice you hear in your "inner ear" is just not the way you're coming across.

Listen to yourself speak when you're alone. Try to describe the voice you hear in a few words. Without revealing the words you've selected to describe your voice, ask a classmate to describe your voice in a few words. Compare the descriptions. How much do you and your classmate agree? How do you sound to others?

Your voice is the most versatile instrument you have for communicating your ideas and feelings to other people. Although you may be able to express yourself more skillfully in writing than in speaking, no writing can capture all the powers and shadings of the human voice. Speech, along with gesture, is one of the most economical means of communication we have. In addition to whatever meaning your words carry, think of the various messages you can give a listener by your tone, the rate at which you speak, the use of emphasis, the loudness or softness of your voice. All these clues in your voice tell others a great deal about your moods and feelings. They can help listeners to know whether or not you really mean what your words say.

Whenever you speak, you are an *information source.* Your voice is the *transmitter* that sends out your words (the *message*). Since the words travel through the air, air becomes the *channel* of communication. Someone, a *receiver,* hears your words, and communication may then take place.

If your message is transmitted to your listener and you receive any kind of response, you receive *feedback.* Let's say you ask a friend, "Got a dime?" If your friend gets the message, he may nod, say "Yes" or "No," or turn out the insides of his pockets to show you that he is broke. However, if you've got a bad head cold or if you don't speak clearly or if your friend isn't paying attention, he might think you said "Got the time?" Then, if he looks at his watch and says, "It's getting close to three o'clock," you know that your attempt at communication has gotten fouled up. *Interference* has prevented successful communication.

Communication is, at best, an inefficient process. We are constantly asking each other questions to see how well we understand one another: "Do you get what I mean?" "Do you follow me?" "Do you know who you're talking to?" We watch each other's faces carefully for expressions that will give us clues. We know that a wrinkled brow is an expression of wonder or doubt. A smile generally (but not always) indicates understanding or agreement. A tightening of the lines around the mouth of a listener may indicate we've struck a sensitive chord. We're very often misunderstood when we think we're expressing ourselves clearly. We often cry out, "You don't understand what I'm saying!" and in our frustration to make ourselves understood, we often rephrase our statements or repeat them with different emphasis. Even with people we're closest to, we often cannot communicate what we think and feel.

That's as technical as I'd like to get with you in this book. The process of communication is important to understand, but right now I'm concerned with your getting to know yourself. Fingerprints and voiceprints remind us that we are all unique. Let's assume we all believe it is better to be human and unique than to be mechanical and identical. Of course, it may be hard to recognize your uniqueness, for other people probably treat you most of the time as a member of a group—a family, a class, a club.

It is sometimes easier for me to treat my children as if they are in the group *children* than to treat them as Dave, Ted, and Josh. I sometimes feel, "No son of mine should behave like that," immediately putting the son in question into a group rather than considering him as an individual person. Do you ever feel yourself being treated as a student or daughter or son or friend or citizen or adolescent rather than as the special, particular, individual person that is *you*? I dare say you do feel this way at times, and I dare say you have treated others this way because practical living demands it to a certain degree. However, wouldn't you prefer to be treated as someone with unique fingerprints—or voiceprints? If your answer to that question is *yes,* then you are obliged to seek knowledge of your own prints—and that takes a lot of work. You have to be willing to deal with and live with and respect your own feelings. It may sound easy, but have you really tried it? Usually our feelings are our own secrets and we often hide them, choosing to express other feelings that we think are acceptable, expected, approved, or profitable.

Sometimes we feel more than one way but have to act as if we feel only one way. We become confused and frightened, and end up not knowing what we feel. Feelings become a threat to us, and we begin to fool the world by giving in to our parents, brothers and sisters, teachers, and friends. We tell them only what we think they want to hear. Doing that may leave you confused about your own feelings, or even unsure of what you really feel. Therefore, when someone tells you to write or speak from your own knowledge or experience, you can find yourself at a loss. Confusion about your own feelings can be a great stumbling block to good talk. For that reason, I am encouraging you to carefully consider your feelings about anything as a way to get to know what you already know (but don't know that you know). I'm encouraging you to make contact with yourself.

There are some situations where you know that you are afraid of looking foolish, of failing, of not being liked, of not being an attractive date, of being unimaginative, of hurting someone. Have you ever asked yourself, "How do I make people like me?" Are you sometimes afraid of the anger you may feel toward your parents, toward others at home, toward your teachers or school administrators? Are you ever afraid to tell some of your teachers that you have feelings of distrust, admiration, dislike, or pleasure?

Let me give you an example of my getting to know something I already knew. When I once failed an examination, I asked my friend Clint how he had scored on the test. He answered that he had failed, and suddenly I felt myself smile. I had a similar reaction when a friend of mine once told me he, too, had just received his draft notice. These two experiences taught me that I can know pleasure when another person has some misfortune which I had no part in creating. To know that about myself was not a happy insight because I didn't want to believe I was that rotten. But the truth of the matter is I do have that feeling, and I have to live with it. I later discovered that the Germans have a word for the feeling: *Schadenfreude.* I didn't even want to know that I knew the feeling. Yet I learned that I didn't have to be ashamed of the feeling. I should be ashamed only if I act on the feeling and hurt a person whose misfortune gives me pleasure. Facing that feeling was facing a secret that I had hidden from myself because I wanted to believe that I was a nicer person, and such a feeling didn't go with being nice. But it was, nevertheless, my feeling.

Because we are afraid of getting hurt, we are afraid to believe that we can hurt anyone else. We have to learn to live with the fact that we have many feelings that we would like not to have. When you say to someone, "I could have killed him," you could have somewhere inside you. The fact that you didn't speaks well for your separation of feeling and action, but don't ignore the feeling. Consider any secret feeling you have and face it. Share it with another student, preferably a good friend. Do this outside the classroom. Ask your friend to share a secret feeling with you.

Did you find such a conversation painful? Uncomfortable? Pleasurable? Disgusting? Or were you indifferent? What about your friend?

Can you now begin to consider another secret you have, either among your feelings or your dreams or your fears? Let me tell you a poem I once wrote:

> You only know a man when you know his dreams.
> His troubles tell you only how he lives.
> To discover that which is
> Instead of that which seems,
> Don't ask of his pain,
> Ask of his dreams.

Do you believe what I said in that poem? Do you know your own dreams? Do you know the dreams of your family or friends?

After you begin searching out some of your own dreams, you might try searching your dreams for some of your fears. Take some time to do that searching. It will help you in your power to speak well. It will help you in your power to get participation from others when you speak. For your speech is definitely connected to your knowing something about your own feelings.

Now one of the problems in the search for your own feelings is that you will find you have contradictory thoughts about many situations, people, institutions, and beliefs. You may both like and dislike school, appreciate and fear rules, yearn for freedom yet seek security. You may want to do your homework and at the same time go out on a date. You may want to be with a friend and at the same time feel that you don't want to see that friend. I once saw a girl's diary in which she wrote, "I'm glad Mother didn't let me go away for the weekend," but two days earlier she had argued violently with her mother, insisting that she be allowed to go.

It is this variety of feelings, perhaps too simply called contradictions, that creates serious problems in our communication. With a confusion of feelings that we don't even recognize, our speech can become confused as well. When do you think you talk most clearly? Do you think it is right for me to conclude that you talk most clearly when your feelings are least confused? Willy Sutton, the famous bank robber, was once asked why he robbed banks. He answered, "That's where the money is." A great baseball manager, feeling victory in his grasp, was asked for advice by his next batter. He answered, "Hit 'em where they ain't."

When your feelings are simple, direct, singular, and obvious, it is probable that your speech will come easier. "I'm hungry," or "Dad, I'm scared," or "Mom, get Dad off my back." Can you think of situations or relationships in your life that you can talk about easily, simply because your feelings about them are clear and simple?

Now pick out another situation or relationship that you have mixed feelings about and try talking about it. Do you speak as easily? I asked my son Ted to do what I have just asked you to do. He talked first about skiing, then about his brother David. This is our conversation:

HOWARD STEIN
I want to talk to you about a couple of subjects. There is no right answer or wrong answer. I'm simply interested in hearing how you would describe your feelings or attitudes or thoughts about these subjects.

The first subject I would like you to talk to me about is skiing. If someone were to ask you to talk about skiing, just skiing in general, what would you talk about? What would you want to say?

TED STEIN

That it was fun. And that it's not that hard to learn because a lot of people just don't go skiing, don't like to start skiing, because they think they have to go down all these big hills. But there are beginner's slopes and everything, so they wouldn't have any problems, and they could take ski lessons and everything. It's a lot of fun. And it's a little expensive, but it's fun when you get all your equipment and everything.

HOWARD STEIN

Can you tell me about your brother Davie?

TED STEIN

What about him?

HOWARD STEIN

Well, whatever you would like to say about him. However you feel about him.

TED STEIN

He's a pain in the neck. No, he bothers me a lot, but sometimes he's okay. I don't know. He's kind of mean. He never answers your questions or anything. He also thinks he is a supreme ruler over everything. Stuff like that.

HOWARD STEIN

But that's what he thinks. What do you think?

TED STEIN

I think he's a pain in the neck.

HOWARD STEIN

Is that all you think about him?

TED STEIN

No, I think . . . he's . . . I don't know. He thinks he's . . . I think he thinks he's so much greater than everybody and everything compared to us, especially me and Josh. But I don't know. Sometimes he's okay, but sometimes he bothers me and Josh. I mean, I don't know, you know, what he's like with his friends, you know, because I don't know. He goes out with his friends and everything, and I don't know what he's like with them.

HOWARD STEIN
What kinds of feelings do you think you have about him?

TED STEIN
Well, you know, I don't mind him some of the time. Some of the time I do mind him . . . umm . . . I don't know. Sometimes we get along and sometimes we don't. Most of the time we don't.

I wonder if you share my conclusion about this conversation: Ted speaks best—that is, most directly and with greatest clarity—when his feelings about a subject are least mixed. When talking about skiing, he first speaks of his pleasure, for obviously he has a great deal of fun with the sport. His second thought is an articulated feeling of a fear he once had, a fear that he assumes people such as his brother Josh have about the sport. His speech reflects a desire to minimize that fear and to encourage people to try the sport and overcome their fear. He takes pleasure in his equipment, but he recognizes the money problem that skiing presents. He speaks to his subject.

When it comes to his brother, his predominant feeling is anger ("He's a pain in the neck"), a feeling which is followed by guilt, envy, rage, disgust, and a kind of indirect affection. Because of the variety of these feelings, he has difficulty in being articulate about his brother, although you've probably concluded that Ted feels more displeasure about his brother than pleasure, more disgust and anger than joy and affection. But most feelings are mixed, and a speaker has to concentrate on clarifying them, sorting them out, in order to decide what to talk about. Remember also that being in touch with your own feelings means that you'll be more aware of the changing feelings you have each day. Ted's remarks about his brother might be very different on another day, but they still will be more complex than his feelings about skiing.

Have I talked too much about you and your feelings? Let me stop for now. Remember, my assumption is that you speak best—that is, most directly, with greatest clarity and economy, and with most personal satisfaction—when you know what you are talking about. What you know most about is your own experience, even though much of what you know is hidden in your memory. And that knowledge is in the form of feelings rather than information or thoughts. When it comes to feelings, the task is not to judge them or influence them. The task is to recognize your own feelings. Actions are to be judged, not feelings. Feelings are yours, not because you create them, but simply because, like Mount Everest, they are there.

It takes two to tango.

Common sense tells you that before you can speak to a group of people—whether in a classroom or a courtroom or a lecture hall or at a banquet—you have to learn to speak to another person. Since talking is such a natural activity, we frequently have conversations without realizing that we are engaged in a public rather than a private activity. Two's a crowd.

For instance, think of something you would like to tell a neighbor or friend: "My parents had a fight," or "I couldn't do one of the math problems for homework," or "My sister thinks she's in love." If you tell any of these things to your friend, do you expect an answer? If so, what do you expect your friend to say? If you receive a response from someone, you are in the midst of a conversation.

SPEAK WHEN SPOKEN TO

The first problem in a conversation is the problem of *listening*. You expect your friend to listen to you when you tell what you want to say. At least, I hope you want your friend to listen. Otherwise, you would just be talking to hear yourself talk. And I am sure you have already had the unhappy experience of being forced to listen to people who like to hear only the sounds of their own voices.

Listening is one of the toughest lessons to learn. To really hear someone speak to you means that you have to turn yourself off, to look at the person who is talking to you, and to *concentrate* on what is being said. You listen with your eyes as much as you do with your ears in conversation. Try closing your eyes and listening. Is there a difference in your

What is the sound of one hand clapping?

conversation? Do this with a classmate, either in class or when you're just sitting around after school.

One of my students, Sterling Brinkley, once wrote a little play about a conversation—or rather an attempt at a conversation—that I think you would enjoy reading. Perhaps you've felt like the boy in this play in your own attempts at conversation. The play takes place in a living room after dinner. Father is sitting, smoking a pipe, reading a newspaper. Junior enters and sits in the Big Chair.

Junior: *(Unsure.)* Dad?
Father: *(Reading the newspaper.)* Yeah, son?
Junior: *(Very sincere, and thought out.)* Dad . . . I . . . uh . . . don't feel we . . . uh . . . talk sincerely, er, genuinely, and I think it's about time we got to know each other . . . as friends?
Father: Son! That's a delightful idea. Let us say something Genuine. Mom! Mom! Come here!
(Mom comes into the living room with a dishtowel in her hand.)
Mom: Yes, my darling?
Father: Come here, my peach. Junior and I are going to say something real. I mean sincere. . . .
Junior: Yes, something Genuine.
Mom: *(Stares for a moment, then slowly breaks into tears.)* Why that's . . . that's just . . . that's . . . that's . . . *(In tears, runs to Father's side, kneels by him. Looks beseechingly at Junior.)*
Junior: *(Very sincere.)* Dad. . .
Mom: *(Interrupting.)* Stop. . . .
Father: What is it, dear?
Mom: I . . . think . . . *(Brushes away a tear. In a passion-filled, yet controlled voice)* . . . Herbert?
Father: Yes, dear, I am *listening.*
Mom: *(In a whisper to her husband, as if she is embarrassed at Junior witnessing this show of great passion.)* Let's call the whole family.
Father: *(Loud.)* Call the whole family?
Junior: Great idea, Dad!
Father: Oh, Joanne, Princess! Come to Daddy!
Mom: William!
Junior: Puppydog, come to Junior!
(Joanne, William, and Puppydog all skip merrily in.)

William and Joanne: *(Being very cute.)* Yes, Mawma?
Puppydog: Bow wow, rofroff!
Everybody: Oh, hush, you Bad Dog!
Father: *(Looks very sincerely at each.)* Mom . . . Junior . . . Bill . . . Joanne.
Puppydog: Bow wow.
Father: *(Forces a laugh; big smile.)* And yes, you, *too*, Puppydog. Kids, family . . . I called you here, because Junior and I are going to say something . . . something . . . Sincere . . . something . . .
(Puppydog walks out of the room.)
Everybody: Puppydog.
(Puppydog enters momentarily, then leaves.)
Junior: That dog!
Father: Why, I never!
(Silence.)
Joanne: *(Crying.)* Mommy, I'm thirsty! *(Complete change of attitude.)* I'm gonna get some water *(Exits.)*
Father: Oh, Joanne, get your dadda some too!
(Silence.)
Mom: *(Whispering.)* Go on, dear . . . go on!
Father: We can't go on without our Joanne.
Mom: Whatever you say, Herb.
(Silence. Eventually the sound of the television coming from upstairs can be heard.)
Junior: What's that?
Father: *(Indignant.)* What is what? *(Turns away.)*
Junior: *(Soft.)* Nothing.
Mom: *(Suddenly very excited.)* Oh! Quiet!
William: What is it, Mom?
(Everybody listens intently.)
Mom: That's . . . that's Julia Childs. *(She runs out of the room.)*
William: *(Imitating his mother.)* That's Julia Childs! *(Runs out of the room.)*
Father: *(Laughing silently.)* What a family! *(Starts reading the newspaper.)*
(Silence.)
Junior: *(Soft.)* Dad?
Father: *(Not looking up.)* Yeah, son?
Junior: I thought . . . maybe you . . . maybe just you and me . . .

Father: *I*, son, *I*. You and *I*. *(Pause.)* Yeah?
Junior: No, Dad, it's *me*.
Father: *(Smiles. Very understanding.)* Son . . . grammar hasn't changed that much since my day. It is *I*. *(Begins reading the newspaper again.)*
Junior: *(To himself.)* It's *me*. *(Exits.)*
Father: *(Still reading. Pause. Turns page.)* What is what? Son?

I suspect you would agree with me that the problem Junior has in this play is the problem of listening—or being listened to. You've no doubt felt the same problem and the same feelings of frustration in wanting to hold a conversation with someone who seems to be interested in hearing what you have to say but just doesn't pay attention. And you should ask yourself if you may be guilty of not listening at times.

One of the main problems in conversation is getting to know the person you are talking to. We actually take for granted that we know the person. We simply say, "I put myself in his shoes." No one, however, no matter how smart or sympathetic, can really do that. Some people are better at it than others, but we can never fully know all that's going on in the mind of the person with whom we may be holding a conversation.

Some people are better at having feelings of *empathy* than most of us. For instance, when my son Davie was a little more than two years old, he went to the coffee table, found a cigarette, and started to eat it. I immediately knocked the cigarette from his mouth when I saw what he was doing, and I reprimanded him: "Davie, what in the world are you doing eating a cigarette!" My wife, on the other hand, because she has a greater ability to put herself in someone else's shoes than I do, quietly said to me, "What do you suppose Davie thinks when he sees a cigarette in your mouth getting smaller and smaller? What could you possibly be doing but eating it?" That incident taught me a good lesson.

I have to work very hard to put myself in my children's shoes, just as they have to work very hard to put themselves in mine. None of us succeed except on rare occasions, but our best conversations come when we are aware of how difficult it is to empathize with the other.

At best, we try to know whatever is available for us to know, and because we are so imperfect and so limited, we have all the more reason to be tolerant of one another. After all, we are always acting in ignorance. How can you know what the other person is thinking about when you are talking to him? Let me tell you still another story.

I once taught a class in freshman English to a group of older students who had had a hard time getting out of high school and into college. The subject on this particular day was the semicolon, and I was acting as if the semicolon was the most important thing in the world. I noticed that one of the students, Mr. O'Connor, wasn't paying too much attention, and, after class, I reprimanded him for his conduct. "O'Connor, you haven't been doing the quality of work you are capable of doing," I said to him. "Earlier in the semester you turned in excellent papers, and your contribution in class was first-rate. Lately, you have been sluggish and sloppy." He looked at me and said, "I know, Mr. Stein, and I'm sorry. But my wife left me recently, and as soon as I get my wits together again, I'll do better with the semicolon."

He taught me a good lesson: *Listening is dependent upon a lot of factors.* But, regardless of all the momentary distractions of daily life, what can you do about cultivating the ability to listen? The ability to put yourself in the other person's shoes?

Most important, you can *look* at the person doing the talking. What does that person look like? Good-looking? Pretty? Slight? Heavy? Long hair or short? What color eyes? What kind of clothes? Close your eyes, and describe the person from memory.

By looking closely at the person you are speaking to, you can get some knowledge about how your words are being received. And, if you can't get that knowledge, at least you can receive attention. The speaker and listener look at one another not just to be polite, but to communicate. I don't mean to exaggerate this point, nor to cultivate a classroom of students who go about staring at one another until they are black and blue in the face. What I am asking you to do is to concentrate on listening, on hearing what is being said. Your temptation is probably the same as mine—to let my mind, and therefore my eyes, wander. The only way to counter that temptation is to concentrate deliberately on putting your eyes in line with the speaker's. Look your conversation partner in the eye in order to put your ear at his command. Hear words being spoken to you, not your response. Your response should be made only after you have heard what has been said to you.

I would like to suggest a looking activity for you to try with your classmates. Because you and I cannot see our own eyes, we can only get some sense of how we use our eyes by looking in a mirror. Now, that may be painful, for we do not always like what we see, or we may be too self-conscious about what we see. Nevertheless, it is a worth a try—not for the sake of vanity, but for the sake of looking. Stand in front of a mirror and watch yourself speak, pretending that you are having a conversation with another person. Try to make a strong point, and see how much you communicate with your eyes. If you have ever heard your own voice, you probably were shocked, and possibly failed even to recognize your voice. The same may be true of your appearance in conversation. Do you recognize the speaker in the mirror—the one your friends see every time you hold a conversation?

Now, in class, choose a partner—preferably someone you haven't gotten to know well. Facing your partner, become your partner's mirror image. You should imitate exactly everything your partner does. Without speaking. Let me suggest three things for you and your partner to do, taking turns. First, comb your hair. Then, brush your teeth. And, finally, put on (and tie, if necessary) one of your shoes. Of course, you don't need combs or toothbrushes—or even shoes—to do this. What you are doing is a form of pantomime, which is a very specialized kind of communication. But you don't have to be concerned with that now. What you're really doing is getting to know yourself better by getting to know someone else.

Try this mirroring activity with several partners, and pick your own, everyday actions. See how well you can coordinate your movements. And see how well you look, watch, and see. Although your classmate may be a stranger to you—or may seem like a stranger—that classmate is, in a way, yourself.

An audience is a mirror image of yourself. If what you have to say is interesting to you and if it is presented in a colorful and dramatic way, the chances are that it will be interesting to an audience. Later, when you stand before your classmates to speak to them, remember that earlier you were mirror images, and you'll probably feel more comfortable. And you may want to repeat this activity from time to time, just to keep in touch with your classmates.

Communication between a speaker and listener is a two-way process. To talk successfully with someone doesn't mean that you have to reach agreement. Communication is not the same as agreement. What you have to do is hear your speaker fairly. Hear what he or she *says*, not what you want to hear said.

The reason we often confuse communication with agreement is that we think if we can be heard, we will have agreement. That is just the opposite of the line I used to hear continually when I was growing up: "I hear you talking, but I don't know what you're saying." What do you suppose people were trying to tell me when I was growing up?

My children frequently refuse to talk to me after a short discussion or disagreement on some matter precisely because they claim I am not listening to them. Let me give you a verbatim transcript of just such a conversation that I had with my son Josh this morning:

JOSH STEIN

The shoes Mom bought me stink. They're no good for basketball. I slip all over.

HOWARD STEIN

I have a pair of the same kind and I play with you every Sunday, and I don't slip.

JOSH STEIN

But I do. The shoes I need are the suede kind, and the store has a sale on. Usually they sell for eighteen dollars, but they've been reduced to ten. The ones Mom bought cost only something like three.

HOWARD STEIN

You use sneakers to play basketball with for only one season. Then they're too small. Ten dollars is too much money for them, even if they are suede.

JOSH STEIN

You don't understand. I need them.

HOWARD STEIN

I do understand that you want them, that your teammates would be impressed, and even envious. But I can't afford them.

JOSH STEIN

You never understand. You only want to hear one side, your side. It's not fair. I can't talk to you about anything.

I think we were communicating perfectly. I knew what my son wanted, and he knew what I was saying. Because we disagreed, he interpreted our conversation as being unintelligible: "I can't talk to you about anything." What about you? Can you think of a situation in which you communicated with someone who disagreed with you? Was the exchange a real communication, or did you leave feeling that you had not really talked with each other? Have you ever been in an argument and felt that you and your adversary were genuinely communicating? Do you prefer agreement in your communication? Do you think people are not listening to you when they don't agree with you?

When we talk to people, we make assumptions about them, even if we don't know we are doing that. We first of all assume that we talk the same language. That means not only that we speak English, but that we share common experiences. The most common kinds of experience that we share are feelings of love, envy, laziness, jealousy, ambition, guilt, shame, fear, regret, delight, surprise, disgust, anger, pride. Feelings are the common factor. Experiences we share are not necessarily isolated incidents. Instead, they may be the feelings that go along with a variety of experiences.

You can assume that an audience knows all the feelings I've just mentioned. You can assume that these feelings have been known by people in the audience since they were infants. You can also assume that some words mean very similar things to all of us: *red, spaghetti, baseball.*

But there are many words that we can't be sure will have the same associations for all listeners: *terrific, love, pretty, handsome, good, bad, right, wrong, freedom, square, right on, wow.* Words for which there is a common picture in our minds, like *red* or *spaghetti,* give us a chance to share a similar experience. But words which do not have the power to create a picture in our minds (such as *you know*) do not mean the same thing to all listeners, and the differences are crucial when we try talking to one another. You must be careful about your assumptions when you think your listener has the same frame of reference that you do. We'll come back to this point later, because not having a common frame of reference is the most significant pitfall you can encounter in communication in general and speech in particular. Remember the problem of interference, which can prevent you from getting your message through.

Because talking is so natural for us, we take it for granted. And therefore we can talk without listening. Are you a good listener? How can you tell? Let me give you an activity in listening based on this scene from Shakespeare's *Othello:*

Othello: What dost thou say, Iago?
Iago: Did Michael Cassio, when you wooed my lady,
  Know of your love?
Othello: He did, from first to last. Why dost thou ask?
Iago: But for a satisfaction of my thought,
  No further harm.
Othello: Why of thy thought, Iago?
Iago: I did not think he had been acquainted with her.
Othello: Oh yes, and went between us very oft.
Iago: Indeed!
Othello: Indeed! Aye, indeed. Discern'st thou aught in that?
  Is he not honest?
Iago: Honest, my lord!
Othello: Honest! Aye, honest.
Iago: My lord, for aught I know.
Othello: What dost thou think?
Iago: Think my lord!
Othello: Think my lord!
  By Heaven, he echoes me
  As if there were some monster in his thought
  Too hideous to be shown.

Notice how Iago echoes the last words of Othello and turns the words into implied questions. Try the same technique with an acquaintance. Don't do it in a manner that will make the person angry, which is what Iago is trying to do in his talk with Othello. Simply listen during a conversation with someone you know, and when the person talking to you pauses, take the last words you hear and rephrase them into a question. The chances are that the speaker will try to elaborate on what he had been saying to you. Try the experiment away from the classroom with someone who has not read this book. Report the results to your classmates.

Another very good method of learning how to listen is by interviewing someone. Both the interviewer and the person being interviewed have to be listening to one another. You have already read an interview I had with one of my children. Try a similar interview with one of your friends or with a member of your family. Prepare a few questions such as, "What kind of neighborhood do you live in?" or "Where do you shop?" or "Where do you play?" or "Recall your first teacher in school." In addition to your prepared questions, ask spontaneous questions that come directly from what the person you are interviewing tells you. Those questions may bring the most interesting answers.

What was most difficult about the interview? Were you interested in what was being communicated? Did you communicate anything in the interview, or were you merely a passive listener? Can you interview yourself? I would suggest that you try it. Conduct a one-minute interview of yourself about one aspect of your life such as the community in which you were raised or the family into which you were born or the schools you had to attend or the food you eat or the books you read.

Did you listen to yourself talk? Is there a difference between "liking to hear yourself talk" and "listening to yourself talk"?

One of the secrets of good conversation is that each party must be genuinely interested in what is being said. During the interviews you just did, were you more interested in what you learned during the interview of yourself or what you learned during the interview of your friend or member of your family?

Much conversation you hear may be made simply to fill up silence, for silence is unbearable. Do you feel yourself unworthy of good conversation? Many people feel that way, and as a result they either talk all the time, boring everyone with their silliness, or else they withdraw into silence and hardly speak to anyone. Everyone worries about not having something interesting to say. If you feel that, you are certainly not alone. The important thing is to do something about it. I suggest one single, useful principle: you will speak interestingly about something that interests you. And, in good conversation, you will be listening to the speaker as well as to yourself because you will be interested in what is being said.

No one can listen well to someone whose talk isn't interesting. However, sometimes you have to make yourself listen in order to hear something interesting. That sounds like a contradiction. But remember what I have been saying to you: you have to try listening before you stop listening. You have to exert yourself. You have to give the speaker the benefit of the doubt. That's a lot to ask of you, and I know it. But everyone who has something to say deserves that much sacrifice, if necessary, on the part of an audience. Before you turn the channel on the TV set, you usually watch a little of the show. Try doing the same with people you talk to. And remember that listening is not just standing. Listening is hearing. You surely have experienced that painful time when people to whom you were talking didn't listen to you. Don't forget that when someone is talking to you.

Making Contact with Kurt Vonnegut, Jr.

Before you begin some speaking activities, perhaps you would like to read the conversation I held with Kurt Vonnegut, Jr. It is a conversation about language—its value, its work, its difficulty. I think you'll enjoy it. The conversation was recorded in New York City in August of 1972. You have perhaps read novels by Kurt Vonnegut, Jr., including *The Sirens of Titan, Mother Night, Cat's Cradle, Slaughterhouse-Five*, and *Breakfast of Champions* (which had just been completed when we talked together). You may also have seen his play or the film version of *Happy Birthday, Wanda June*, and the film version of *Slaughterhouse-Five*.

photo by Jill Krementz

STEIN

I would like to find out how you feel about language—the value of language, the work of language, the difficulty of language.

VONNEGUT

You should understand that I was trained in the use of language by managers of an industry which no longer exists, the short story industry. The managers of this industry had certain rules about language in stories which I had to learn. These managers, these editors, required that whenever a character spoke in a story, what he said had to either advance the story or reveal something significant about the character. The demand was for efficiency. I learned that lesson so well and it is so automatic with me now when I write that when a character speaks he either advances the story or reveals something significant about himself, or he does not speak. This makes for efficiency; I don't know whether it makes for art. Anybody who follows those rules will write a story which moves faster, which is more exciting to the reader.

STEIN

When you wrote those stories, was the language easy to come by, or did you have to struggle over the words?

VONNEGUT

It was easy to come by because there were many models around. I would read other authors who were writing for the same magazines—some of the great men like Faulkner and Hemingway and Fitzgerald and John O'Hara. And let me say parenthetically: there's one thing which adds to a story which is not put in a story—the reputation of the author himself. After Hemingway became famous and people knew a lot about his life, his every character was Hemingway speaking. When I started out, and nobody had heard of me, I worked hard at dialect. I worried about the vocabularies of different characters, whether a person with this background or that background would know a particular word. I have stopped doing that now because here I am, fifty years old, and everybody knows it is me speaking anyway. The critic Wilfrid Sheed wrote about what leaving this country does to the writing of authors. And he offered the gloriously impudent suggestion that Hemingway's style was a result of Hemingway's having been away from America so long that he did not know how they spoke there anymore.

So he chose what other people have called "explosive baby talk"—small words, simply constructed sentences—because he was not confident enough about the sound of American speech anymore.

STEIN

Couldn't hear it anymore.

VONNEGUT

Couldn't hear it. I think I have a tin ear now because it no longer matters that I reproduce speech. It matters that I reproduce me, and that has to do with where a person is in his career.

STEIN

But, Kurt, you're an awfully good listener. I've been around you a long time, and I think you must hear very well now.

VONNEGUT

Yes, but I'm not a good mimic. I think what I hear are people's attitudes and not their manners of speech. I can't imitate people well. I do not have a good ear for languages, so I'm not a good mimic. My dialogue is not particularly to be admired. But I hear people's attitudes, yes.

STEIN

Do certain kinds of voices turn you off?

VONNEGUT

Yes, but I suppose that has to do with my childhood, with resonances of people I didn't like in childhood. It seems to me that people are more conscious of how they speak now. It seems to me that ten or twenty years ago, people hurt each other's ears more. When I got into the army, a southerner said to me, *Do you have to talk like that? It hurts my ears.* I talked Indiana talk the way everybody talked in high school out in Indianapolis. Our teacher said it was dictionary English. But it hurt the southerner's ears, so I stopped doing it. And most people out there have stopped doing it.

STEIN

You're talking now about dialect and sound and rhythm more than particular words characters use. In your play, *Happy Birthday, Wanda*

June, I recall that when there was a confrontation between the returning hero and his wife, and between the hero and his son, there was a lot of good exchange. Now, is that just by chance, or are you willing to acknowledge that you gave them individual voices?

VONNEGUT

No, they do have their individual voices, but they're a matter of attitude, not of sentence length or vocabulary. I was able to make the hero use flowery words, to speak ornately: that requires no skill. One problem with the play is that everyone got to speak his piece, and the orchestration of plays, and of books too, in the past has been to let one character speak a lot more than the other characters, to be onstage a lot more and to say the best things. I'm trying to get away from that.

STEIN

In what sense, Kurt?

VONNEGUT

I'm trying to give everyone a fair shake. In my new book, *Breakfast of Champions,* every character has a value equal to every other character. And I argue in the book that an awful lot of the mistaken attitudes that human beings have had, *cruel* attitudes, grow from the way stories have been told—not out of viciousness, but out of dramatic necessity.

STEIN

Could you give me an illustration of that?

VONNEGUT

Yes. We believe that noblemen are noble rather than simply people at the top of society, and this has been so in theaters for a long time. It's a convenient way to put on a play. It's a convenient attitude to hold in a theater, but it's a very inconvenient one, an unfair one, to hold in real life. We are taught, simply because of the way we've told stories, that there are some people who do not matter. These are the bit-part players.

STEIN

A principal rule of the theater is that there are no bit parts, but we know that there are.

VONNEGUT

Well, of course. I mean, the audience knows it needn't watch some characters too much because they are obviously expendable. There are some characters who must survive through the end of the final act. Others may die. Chess is organized in this way. Chess is a game. But it also serves as a social model where it was never intended to.

STEIN

Someone once asked an author how he was able to write a woman. And he said, *I simply put myself in her place.* It's always been a mystery to me how an author can give a voice to another person.

VONNEGUT

I've avoided writing about women until very recently because women had not been candid with me until very recently, and only recently have I discovered that their heads are just like mine.

STEIN

In *King Lear,* Shakespeare has Lear describe his daughter's voice as *soft, gentle, and low, an excellent thing in woman.* Do you think that men and women have traditional vocal roles, and, if so, do you think these roles are changing?

VONNEGUT

I remember when we were young there were very few women who appeared at political conventions. We would listen to them on the radio, and whenever Frances Perkins and Eleanor Roosevelt spoke, their voices were harsh and embarrassing. You had the feeling that they did not belong on radio and really did not belong at the conventions. I went to the 1972 Republican Convention and I heard a lot of women speak, and they probably understand microphones much better now than they did then. They didn't hurt my ears. People have had an awful lot of voice training on the telephone, you realize. You learn a technique because there's feedback from the instrument, so the telephone's a teaching machine as far as speaking pleasantly goes.

STEIN

When you go about creating a Trafalmadore in a novel, there's a world outside of my world. And yet the people who inhabit that world are somewhat recognizable to me. The only way you can create such a world is through the language. The words have made it. There's nothing physical out there. It's on a page, and you bet everything on those words as the only instruments you have. That fascinates me.

VONNEGUT
Yes, but you yourself have done it. I think it is astonishing that you can count on strangers to take symbols off a page, little black marks on a white page, and to give the characters dialect, to costume them, to build sets, to be in countries that the reader has never been before. The printed word is an elitist form because the skills that a reader must bring to a book are extraordinary.

STEIN
And the writer has to count on those skills, doesn't he?

VONNEGUT
Yes, and for that reason he's never going to reach more than, I would suppose, 5 percent of his population, 5 percent of an ordinary western world population. Very few people can read that well. When I make jokes, I'm absolutely dependent on the reader going fast, because I'm going to trip him—that's how my joke works. I'm suddenly going to switch direction, and I'm dependent on making him go headlong in one direction, thinking he knows what's going on as his eyes flick over the words, and all of a sudden, I trip him. I've faked him out; I've switched. And that's a joke. But if a person reads a few words and then goes back to make sure he's got those words right, he'll never get the joke. Because he's just stepped carefully over whatever hazard I've put in his way and never noticed.

STEIN
One hears often now that words are not quite as significant as they may once have been, that we have other means of expressing ourselves —nonverbal communication between people that no longer requires words. Do you think the printed word may die out?

VONNEGUT
What I have to say about that has to do with being a member of a free society. A book is cheap, and an effect such as the end of *Cat's Cradle*,

which was the end of the world, cost me a fraction of a penny to create, counting the paper and the wear on the typewriter ribbon. To make a film out of it would have cost millions. So, if the printed word does die out, it will be bad news for our society. It will be bad news politically because it will mean that only rich people can speak. I treasure the book for political reasons. A book is more of a social act than film, too: it's in the nature of a handshake. Anybody who can read a book well brings an enormous amount of skill and a lot of himself to the job, and so it is a social event. Any book is an entirely subjective experience. Who knows what anybody makes of it? The queer things that books do have no explanations.

STEIN

Such as?

VONNEGUT

People think I'm a short man. They have read my books, and they are all surprised by how tall I am. How I implied shortness, I do not know, but I have come across this so often that it's in my books somewhere. I write like a short man.

STEIN

In my own work with students, I'm not convinced that there's the faith in the word that I was raised with. I was raised to believe for the most part what I read. I was raised to believe that when people spoke, they were telling the truth. My assumption was that if you could *say* it, you had a chance to make an exchange with another person. There was a great emphasis upon the use of words in my family, not just to relieve silence, but to make the family lives richer and happier. I'm not so sure that faith is around now.

VONNEGUT

Conversations between young people today are no worse than ours, but they're different. Each young person gets to perform. You and I learned to talk as if conversation were a ping-pong game, and what I've seen more and more is that one person in a group gets to, in effect, sing his or her song, and then the next person does. The units of exchange are larger. Young people will exchange words in clumps of five hundred, say, where we were taught to exchange them in bunches of twenty, maybe. But we were certainly innocent people, believing everything that was said. And that's over. There aren't many people like that left. After the Second World War, my great buddy Bernard B. O'Hare, who's in *Slaughterhouse-Five,* became a district attorney in Pennsylvania. I asked him one time, *O'Hare, what did the World War II experience do to you? What did you learn from it?* And he said, *I will never believe what my government says anymore.* Before the war he had.

STEIN

There's a character in *Henry IV,* a waiter named Francis, who runs around all the time, picking up glasses and filling them, and he is constantly being called on by the people in the tavern. All he can say is, *Anon, anon, sir. Anon, anon, sir.* At one point the Prince says, *That ever this fellow should have fewer words than a parrot, and yet the son of a woman!* Somehow he can't believe that a human being would be confined to so few words, for the humanizing quality of man is in language, in our being able to speak. Does that make sense to you, or would you prefer to have more silence, fewer words around you?

VONNEGUT

I have heard few people speak charmingly. When I was a child in Indianapolis, the talk I heard was harsh, practical, not playful at all. The Irish, of course, are used to melody around them all the time. And I've heard how outraged the blacks and Puerto Ricans in New York are that their teachers are telling them to be quiet all the time. It's one of the things they can do awfully well—they can talk marvelously, whimsically, majestically. And they never get a chance to do that. When I taught at Harvard, I had a good student named Jerry Hyatt, and we had mimeographed his story and passed it around. People were talking about it, and he got impatient. He said, *Let me read it, let me read it.* And he stood up and, as he read it out loud, he became part of the story. He had written the story feeling very strongly that he was part of it and, in essence, he *sang* it. And it was immaculate; it was *perfect* when Jerry Hyatt performed it.

STEIN

You once said that art and astrology both use fraud in order to make human beings seem more wonderful than they really are. You said that films and books and plays show us people talking much more entertainingly than people really talk. Are you saying, then, that nothing spontaneous is as good as something prepared and rehearsed?

VONNEGUT

No. Because there's usually not enough passion in life to provide the energy for somebody to speak well. But a person in a crisis will speak well. I was at a literary festival at Notre Dame that everybody remembers as a stunning experience. Everybody was talking much better than he ordinarily talked, and there was greater unity between the audience and the people on the stage. And what had happened was that Martin Luther King had been shot, and we were drawing energy from that. Everybody was playing over his head. But ordinarily people aren't passionate; their bodies couldn't stand it if they were all the time, so it's better to prepare something that would simulate the passion.

STEIN

Is there something that charms you in language, just in words themselves?

VONNEGUT

Oh, yes. When somebody speaks well, I'm enchanted, and that can happen even at dinner. I am charmed by some words. I hear someone else use one, and I promise myself to use it, too. A word like *treachery* —I just have to use that somewhere, it's such a great word. I had lunch with Eudora Welty, and I said to her, *You used the word* blunder *twice in your book.* And she had no idea that she had. She wrote about a man walking along *blunderingly.* I said, *That's a perfect word for the way this man is walking.* I was so charmed by it, and it stuck in my mind. I really must use this language more than I have. We have a language which, I think, is twice as large as any other language. That often isn't mentioned. We have the biggest vocabulary in the world, *by far.*

STEIN

Do your characters ever say things that surprise you?

VONNEGUT

Yes. It happened in *Breakfast of Champions.* It's partly about an art festival out in the Middle West. They've had no art out there so far, and they've built this art center which is very expensive. The first acquisition costs one hundred thousand dollars. It's by a young New York painter named Rabo Karabekian. It's a yellowish-green, vertical stripe on a large blue field which is about twelve feet on each side—a huge canvas. Karabekian is there for the opening of the art festival, and he gets into an argument. There have been editorials in the paper about the use of one hundred thousand dollars in this way, even though a local industrialist put up the money. There's bitterness about this. *How could it possibly be worth one hundred thousand dollars?* In a Holiday Inn, he has an argument with a waitress who tells him that at least she hasn't swindled people by selling them a stripe for one hundred thousand dollars. And the whole place becomes silent, waiting for his defense. And I've read defenses of painters of this kind in the *Times* every Sunday, or in art magazines, but I was unsatisfied with what they said. But when Karabekian, my own invention, was through telling these people what a great painting it was and why it was, he not only persuaded everybody in the Holiday Inn, he persuaded me! And I had been out to get him while I was writing the book.

STEIN

So the book wrote itself?

VONNEGUT

No. *Breakfast of Champions* is a labored book. It is not a cry from the heart, so the words didn't arrive—I had to shop around for them. But there are occasions when the human being is sufficiently concerned, sufficiently passionate, and it just all comes out. The mind knows exactly how to put the whole thing together. That's the case in that one great speech in the Holiday Inn.

STEIN

Today we're bombarded with words. I sit in front of a television set for a very short while and I am being bombarded with words as well as with pictures. I'm being satiated with language, which tends to turn me off a little bit. Now, my children, who are between twelve and seventeen, have been raised with that kind of bombardment. And I don't know how much they enjoy playing with words, how much they enjoy savoring words, how much they enjoy the limits, as well as the extensiveness, of words.

VONNEGUT

Your children may like the array of tools that the English language is. They may enjoy it for its own sake. It's certainly a very pretty and amusing thing. What they are really skillful at is detecting sincerity or insincerity. They can tell when somebody says something that really matters to the person who is saying it.

STEIN

You are a playwright, as well as a novelist and short story writer. You've seen your words spoken by people on a stage instead of being read in privacy. That must be quite an experience—for a writer of fiction to suddenly have someone on a stage speak the words and then have an audience receive those words. Now, this has also happened to you in films, and I wonder if it's in any way offended you, if it's pleased you, if it's delighted you?

VONNEGUT

It's excited me. It hasn't been a completely successful experience, so I haven't been gratified. I saw my play onstage, and our cast became very skillful. They became like the Harlem Globe Trotters—they knew every laugh that was there, and they got every laugh. And they also amused each other. We went for over a hundred performances, so the cast got to know the play very well, got to know how the audience would respond. And then I saw the film made of many of those lines. I hated the film because it was a misrepresentation of my attitudes. I watched the film run off in a theater, and I saw the lines lost in the laughter of the audience. The way to make a joke is to rig it: you make a joke and top it. In the movie theater, the audience would laugh at the first joke and not hear the topper. It broke my heart. The joke could not build on film. Perhaps this is one argument for the older and cheaper forms, such as the play and the book: it is possible to time them.

STEIN

Do you think the power of speaking well is just a natural power that people catch and are sort of brought up with? Or do you think that to speak well one must deliberately go about cultivating the power in his life?

VONNEGUT

I think that we should all take lessons in how to speak well most of the time. As it is now, because of the way we have been raised and educated, we can speak well only in moments of passion—which is fortunate, in a way. It's nice to know that you can count on yourself to speak well and clearly in moments of crisis. But most of the people I know are sort of swan-song people who speak well only *in extremis*, and otherwise keep their mouths shut.

STEIN

If you were able to sit in a room with a small group of young people and language was the subject, is there anything special you would want to tell them?

VONNEGUT

I would say to them, *Please charm me with language*, because it may not have occurred to them that such a thing is possible, but it can be done. Younger people find us rude in a lot of ways, and we find them rude in a lot of ways. It's interesting to watch older men like William Buckley or David Susskind leading a show, and seeing the outrage they produce in younger people. They do not know how rude they are being, the older people. And we do not know either because, as I say, we were taught to converse as though it were a game of ping-pong. Younger people believe, and properly so, that a person should be able to speak for a little while, to sing a whole song, in order to express himself.

STEIN

If you were to say something for a period of three or four minutes, and then I were to say something for three or four minutes, I'd assume that this would not be an exchange but, instead, two individuals just expressing themselves. Now, you indicate to me that you really see that as communication going back and forth rather than simply individual expression. But communication is assumed to be a dialogue between people, not two monologues.

VONNEGUT

You and I once believed in progress. We thought that we could actually progress through conversation, could arrive at higher forms of truth through talk. I don't think young people feel that we can get very far with conversation anymore. We're not trying to build stairways to heaven anymore, and we used to do it in all sorts of ways.

STEIN

What are we trying to build then?

VONNEGUT

Links between ourselves based on candor. I was lecturing at Ohio State one time, talking about the American novel and about the size of the English language and all these things we've been talking about. Then I told the audience that when a book is published the author customarily gets six copies, and I said, *I always feel guilty when I get that package.* It was just an aside, you know. But they wanted me to stop there. *Why do you feel guilty?* And I said, *I don't know, I don't like to open it. It's a personal matter.* And I went on with my talk. But they came back to it again and said, *How can anything be that personal?* And I said, *Well, it is.* Then there was a pause, and I said, *Well, all right, I'll tell you.* And I told them this: I'd never told anybody before that my mother was insane at times and it was a family secret, and we managed to keep it a secret. But I was the youngest kid, and the family was scared to death that I would be the leak. A big pressure was brought on me not to tell, not to tell, not to tell. Whenever I get those packages from the publishers, I think what I feel is, *You told, you told.*

The Truth shall make you free.

The most embarrassing, sometimes even disgusting, talkers are people who don't know what they're talking about. You must know many people like that. We all do. Because we believe that all people are entitled to their own opinions, we often talk on subjects we know very little about. We confuse opinions and knowledge. When I begin to predict the football winners for my children, they tell me I don't know what I'm talking about, and usually they are right. When they tell me math is stupid, I tell them they don't know what they are talking about.

SAY IT WITH SPECIFICS

We can't know all that we would like to know. Even information on subjects that interest us greatly may be hard to come by. But we can know more than we usually do. Robert Frost once said that the trouble with being a human being is that you have to act on insufficient evidence. Do you understand what he meant by that? Can you give an illustration from your life of a time when you acted on insufficient evidence? Would you accept the statement that some evidence is more insufficient than other evidence? How would you explain such a statement?

Talk with your classmates about an incident in which you acted on slight evidence. Then discuss another incident when you had more substantial evidence before acting. For example, you might talk about selecting a movie, striking at a pitched ball, ordering a meal in a restaurant, accepting a date, calling a play in football, accepting an invitation, taking a job, deciding whether or not to smoke.

All I want are the facts, ma'am.

Information is tough to come by. What do you consider yourself to be informed about? How did you become informed? What would you like to be informed about? How can you go about getting that information?

Everyone knows that it is necessary to work in order to be informed. There is no easy way. You are surrounded by sources of information every day—news magazines, digests, TV documentaries, rumor, gossip —that attempt to help you stay in touch with the world. But none of these sources of information can really help you keep up with everything. To really know something about the government, your neighborhood, professional baseball, airplanes, poverty in the cities, atomic energy plants, the history of the Indians in America, ecology, the truth about drugs or alcohol or TV, the proper way to raise children, women's liberation—takes a bundle of energy. Maybe you're tempted to say, "Forget it. I'll go along with what I know." But don't you feel, inside, that you don't know enough?

Earlier I said you can't *know* your listeners, but you can make assumptions about them. You can act as if you know them. But when you're dealing with facts—with objective material—you can't make assumptions. What do you know about your representative's voting record in Congress, the organization of a professional basketball league, the training of a high school principal, internal combustion engines, the theory of relativity, the history of marriage, natural childbirth, the Dow Jones average, marketing research?

To know what you're talking about, you must work at getting information. You have to know where to go, what to look for, and what to use. Your information is certain to be less than complete, but it is also certain that you will know more about a subject after you seek information than you did before your search began. Good talk is expensive; cheap talk is cheap. When you don't know the subject you're talking about, yet want to talk about that subject, you have to go out and get information. For most of us, that move may seem like too much trouble. For some of us, however, it is absolutely essential because it contributes to the richness of our lives.

The quality of your life is dependent upon your willingness to find out what you are talking about. You need facts. But you only need facts if you *need* to know what you are talking about. If you are content in going along with rumor, gossip, and conjecture, you will not need to seek information. But if you don't want to be guilty of being simply glib, or even phony, you will try to locate information.

Take one subject: how your janitor got his job, how the weather forecaster determined his predictions for the next day, how your parents came to live in your hometown, how your local library is organized, how the taxes in your community are used. Collect the facts and report your findings to your classmates. Do the same with one of these subjects: hiccoughs, sneezing, yawning, termites, the manufacturing of hot dogs, the origin of playing cards. You can add to the list if you want to. I hope you know that by now, since I have been encouraging you in this book to be on your own.

I may have made you a little nervous about getting information. I hope so, because I think we all need to be jostled into seeking facts and information, just as we need to be jostled into being specific in conversations. Because so many of us are sometimes sloppy, negligent, and ill informed, we frequently find people who use facts or speak with specifics to be somewhat upsetting. They may make us feel uncomfortable or inferior or even dumb. Our defense against them is usually to mock them or to consider them square, dull, and boring. I would caution you not to fall into that trap. It is a trap that can make your life dull and uninteresting.

The know-nots like to keep people around them knowing nothing. Since it is too much of an effort for know-nots to get information (the usual excuse is that they don't have time to read), they try to keep everyone else uninformed. I would advise you to fight them, whether they are your parents, friends, relatives, or teachers. (Remember how difficult it was to get them to tell you the facts of life?) Of course, I would advise you to fight know-nots with politeness, because I believe there seldom is an excuse for being offensive. And I would remind you that you can't fight someone for having insufficient information if you don't first have the information yourself.

I believe you should learn to request, seek, and even demand information. And, again, let me remind you how important it is to learn to separate facts from rumor, gossip, or opinion. You have already had enough experience in life to know the value of facts. What you may not have is the habit of seeking and using facts effectively. My wish is that you begin to demand facts first from yourself, then from the people around you. By seeking out information, you begin to discriminate between intelligent communication, which has value, and statements that are absurd or illogical.

If you have nothing to say, it probably doesn't matter how you say it. But I believe that each of you has something to say, and therefore it matters a great deal how you say it. I would urge you to learn to say it with specifics.

If you think facts are hard to come by, try specifics. Specifics are examples or illustrations, and sometimes resemble facts. For example, have you ever had the following conversation after you brought a friend home to meet your family?

You: How did you like my friend?
Them: We didn't like him.
You: Why not?
Them: We don't know. We just didn't.
You: What didn't you like?
Them: We don't know. Just something about him.
You: WHAT?
Them: It's hard to say. But something is just not quite right about him.

If you've ever had a conversation like that one, you know something about the frustration of seeking specifics. In that conversation, you were the one looking for specifics. However, parents have the same problems with their children. Does this sound familiar?

Us: Where are you going?
You: Out.
Us: Out where?
You: Just out.
Us: When will you be back?
You: Soon.

Us: When?
You: Sometime later.

You know that kind of conversation, too. And you also know the use of the following words: *terrific, far-out, ridiculous, neat, fascinating, great, nice, interesting, weird, cool, you know, stupid.* Not one of those words can tell a listener much, but think how often those words are used. How often do you use them?

I'd like to offer you two examples of how specifics can alter, and even complete, communication. Years ago, I was rehearsing a student-written play about a family who lived on a Nebraska farm. The scene took place in the kitchen where two brothers were celebrating their reunion after having been separated for five years. The older brother looked around the kitchen and said, "This house is the same house it's always been." The actor playing that brother stopped the rehearsal and said to me, "I don't know how to say that line. I don't know what it means." The writer was standing beside me, and said, "It means what it says: the house is the same house it's always been." "But *what's* the same?" asked the actor. The writer paused, heard the intelligence of the question, and said, "I'll tell you tomorrow at rehearsal." And, indeed, the writer did tell him, for at the rehearsal the next day the line read, "This house is the same house it's always been: the same old cookie jar; and look at that crazy excuse for a slop bucket." With those two specifics, the actor then knew how to say the line.

Another illustration comes from a play by Saul Bellow called "The Wrecker." In the play, a woman and her mother are talking about the woman's dilapidated apartment:

Mother-in-law: . . . You shouldn't be sorry to leave this . . . dump. It ought to have been condemned years ago.
Wife: Oh, I'm not exactly sorry. After fifteen years in the same place, though, you stop criticizing it. You never think whether it's a bad place or a good one.
Mother-in-law: Nonsense. You ought to be happy to move into an elevator building. And get rid of the old dumbwaiter. And have white woodwork. And a toilet where you don't have to pull the chain. Things a person needs for her self-respect.

How has Saul Bellow used specifics to make concrete the vague description of the apartment as a "dump"?

The secret of arriving at specifics is to ask questions. The best questions are the ones newspapermen use all the time—who, what, when, where, why, how—because they know that their readers want specifics. Do you use specifics very often? Let me ask you *what* you like about your house? *Why* do you have the kind of car you have in your family? *Who* are your friends? When you say, of a friend, "We just can't communicate," you have to follow that with, "Communicate what?" If you can answer the what, you have arrived at a specific. If you say, "I'm afraid," the next step is to ask, "Afraid of what?"

Just as it is difficult to know a specific feeling, so is it difficult to find a specific illustration that will explain a feeling or thought or even a condition. In the novel *When She Was Good*, Philip Roth describes a time in the life of Roy Bassart in the following way:

> When young Roy Bassart came out the service in the summer of 1948, he didn't know what to do with his future, so he sat around for six months listening to people talk about it. He would drop his long skinny frame into a big club chair in his uncle's living room and instantly slide half out of it, so that his Army shoes and Army socks and khaki trousers were all obstacles to cross over if you wanted to go by. . . .

Another way of writing that second sentence would be to say, "Roy sat in the chair while visiting his uncle." In my sentence, you have no picture at all, while Philip Roth's writing gives you a detailed picture because of all the specifics he has given you to assemble. At the end of the chapter introducing Roy Bassart, Roth doesn't write, "Roy bought a car." Instead, he writes, "Roy . . . bought a two-tone, second-hand 1946 Hudson." I assume that you see what specifics can do, and I hope that I am persuading you to use them more often.

Now, once again, I would like to warn you that people you know might get nervous, even angry, when you begin to badger them for specifics. I once had an unpleasant moment when I first came home from the army, after having been all over Europe. I was told by a member of my family, who had never been out of the United States, "I don't know why, but I love this country." I asked, "Why?"—meaning, "What do you love?"—and the response I got was a cold stare of anger which I have never forgotten. People don't like to be put on the spot, to be required to offer particulars when they want to give generalizations instead. But for the purpose of intelligent and satisfying communication, specifics are a must. They not only illustrate the point being made, but they also show consideration for your listener.

Specifics provide your listener with a picture, a frame of reference. They offer a concrete image, and then your listener has a chance to agree or disagree, approve or disapprove of the image. Your listener is not in the dark. When you use sentences such as, "Was that terrific? I mean far-out, man? I mean fantastic, you know, I mean that's it!" what have you communicated? How often do you find yourself talking like that?

Now, I have told you that the secret to finding specifics is in asking questions. But you may have lost the habit of asking questions. Children are notorious for asking questions because their world consists only of specifics. They are also very concrete and particular in their expression. For example, it is more likely that a child will say, "Me, milk," than "Me drink." Children think in specifics. If you don't believe me, watch a child roll a ball. The child behaves as if each roll is unique, particular, and eternal.

The curiosity of children, and their search for specifics, is something that we tend to knock out of them because of the inconvenience that so often accompanies the questions. I once saw a five-year-old sitting with his father in the rear seat of a Fifth Avenue bus in New York City. As the bus went past Rockefeller Center the child saw the statue of Atlas holding up the world on his shoulders. The child must have been startled by that specific sight, and he turned quickly to his father and said, "Daddy, is that God?" I thought it was a good question: Who else would be able to hold up the world on his back? But the father was embarrassed and told the child to get away from the window. Somehow I have never forgotten that little boy, because I think he must have been taught to stop asking questions. Perhaps his imagination was locked away.

Let me tell you another story. A seven-year-old was home one morning with a cold, and I was his baby sitter. During a moment of great confidence in me, he turned and asked me a secret question: "Hal, see my little canary in the cage?" I answered that I did. The child said, "Do you think that birdie knows he's a little birdie? Does a dog know that he's a dog? I know a tree doesn't know it's a tree, and I know I'm a human being because my mommy told me, but do you think the little birdie knows he's a little birdie?" The specific sight of the bird that inspired the question led to more general thoughts—about dogs, trees, human beings. The bird caught his eye and aroused his curiosity, just as the Atlas caught the eye of the child in the bus.

I didn't tell you how I answered the question about the canary. I did that on purpose. What would you have said to the seven-year-old? To the five-year-old? How specific could you have been?

Remember, in any conversation, the more pictures you can arouse in your listener's mind, the more specific you can be. And your conversation will be clearer for it. You may want to practice some ways of getting specifics, beginning with times when you are alone. How would you put into words what you feel or think or see? In conversation with your friends, how clearly can you communicate by using specifics? And—taking that final step—how well do you know your way around the school library, or any other place where information is stored away for you?

The Truth is in the telling.

Now it's time to get down to the business of making a speech. You've already been sharing secrets, thinking about yourselves, doing interviews, reporting to your classmates. I assume you are getting to know each other rather well, and this is a good time for you to demonstrate some of the things you have been learning.

SPEAK FOR YOURSELF

Making a speech before an audience is like putting on an act. All of us are constantly putting on acts, even if we don't like to always believe it. The poet T. S. Eliot has a character in one of his poems say, "There will be time, there will be time/ To prepare a face to meet the faces that you meet." Although none of us may like to think that we prepare different faces for different people (because that seems a bit phony), the fact is that we do indeed prepare a different face for parents, teachers, friends, clergymen, employers, children, and grandparents. You name it, and we have done it. And this is not because we are phonies, mind you, because we don't intend to lie to any of these people. It is simply that different situations demand different approaches by all of us. Your real face—the one you discover in the mirror—is not the one you always show in different speaking situations.

When you want to impress a boy or a girl, you watch your behavior, and your face shows that kind of care. When you want approval, you behave in a way that you hope will assure your success. No one can prepare a face that is not, in some way, his own. But all of us have a thousand faces to present to the world.

God made man because he loves stories.

By this time you may be in angry disagreement with me. I hope you will argue the case before your teacher and fellow students if that is your feeling. All of us, I contend, are actors, some of us more so than others.

Speaking before an audience is simply an extension of speaking to another person. Tell your class about the day you learned something. Was telling the story to your class the same as telling it to one person? Or different? Perhaps you'd rather tell your classmates another kind of story. Consider talking about one of the happiest days of your life, or one of the saddest days. Don't take just a fairly happy day or just a fairly sad day, but take an *extreme* day. When you choose a topic that you feel strongly about, you have a better chance to be effective. You have more at stake because you are talking about intense, personal feelings. If you can't honestly think of a day that was the happiest or the saddest, your speech won't sound genuine. And I think that you wouldn't be as effective talking about an ordinary day.

I recall the day I went to my first major league baseball game in 1932 as one of the happiest days of my life. I remember the day my mother went to the hospital as one of the saddest days of my life. You, too, have all sorts of material in your memories. Look inside, and pull out the memory that will interest your audience. When your memories and feelings are strong, you won't have to add to your act. You will be an actor, because you will be recalling an event and reporting it as an actor does onstage, pretending that you are reliving that day again by telling your classmates about it. You won't have to worry about livening up what you say when you are very much involved with a story or experience or idea that you are presenting.

Speakers usually appear before a group because they know more about a particular subject than the other members of the group do. Is there any subject that you think you could prepare as a speech to your class precisely because you know more about it than others do? Being a busboy? A waitress? Burying a dog? Moving away from friends? Visiting a foreign land? Taking a watch apart and putting it back together again?

Although I have encouraged you to speak many times to your teacher and your classmates in an informal manner, I am now asking you to consider a more formal presentation. I would like to offer you a little formula for a formal presentation:

> Tell them what you want to tell them.
> Tell them.
> Tell them what you told them.

Obviously, the same principles that we talked about in informal speaking operate in a formal speaking situation: you must know what you are talking about, you must know your feelings about your material, you must be specific, and you must be aware of your audience. The difference between formal and informal speaking is really just a matter of organization. And organization will come more easily if you take the time to plan ahead.

In organizing your speech, think about a beginning, a middle, and an end. Although you may not think so, the middle is the most difficult part to locate. But before we talk about finding middles, let's start with the beginning.

Beginnings are difficult, even embarrassing, on *all* occasions, especially on a date. Starting a conversation (finding openers) is tough for everyone. Try this with someone you don't know, either boy to girl, or girl to boy: "Haven't I seen you on TV?"

Since you have time to prepare a formal speech outside the classroom, you can think long and hard for openers, and you can approach your class with a polished beginning. Questions are excellent beginnings. I recall a young Greek boy in my college class who interrupted a debate one evening when he walked to the front of the room and addressed the audience with the following question: "Do you know what is dying? Do you? Do you know what is dying?" He was outraged at the debate on the Truman doctrine, and he wanted to arouse the audience. He succeeded to the point that the debate was called off, for he launched into such a furious attack on the American political system that the chairman of the debate was forced to conclude the session.

Most of us have forgotten about asking questions, as we discussed in the last chapter. We're often embarrassed to ask them. But questions are arousers, natural arousers, for they need an answer to conclude the attempt at conversation. Asking questions makes your audience interested because each listener has to think of responses. Between the question and the silent answer, there is bound to be expectation and suspense. You break that suspense when you answer your own question (which was then what we call a *rhetorical question,* since you planned on answering it yourself all along), or you may string your audience along, leaving the listeners with the question to answer in their own ways after they've heard you out.

Another opening technique is silence. Because an audience expects a speaker to talk, the speaker can easily capture their attention by saying nothing. That holds the audience in suspense. But I wouldn't exploit that technique. It works on some occasions, mainly when you feel you are having trouble in getting the attention of your audience, but it can also be overused.

The most popular form of beginning a speech is to tell a joke. That kind of beginning has been used so frequently that it is now a cliché and tends to be less effective and less successful than it once was. If your joke has an immediate connection to your subject, I would suggest that you use it. But if the joke is just a means of breaking the silence, I would caution you to be careful and discreet in its use.

Let me choose a subject and start a speech with you. From a list of subjects I would encourage you to examine, I will choose *Walls.* Incidentally, here is the list of subjects:

    Walls
    Doors
    Windows
    Cars
    Chairs
    Lamps
    Words
    Streets
    Books
    Ducks
    Speeches

I first consider what associations I have with walls. Walls make up the rooms I live in, wake in, work in, sleep in, have fun in, suffer in, play in, sit in, read in, walk in. They also make me think of the barriers that people put up between one another. Geography puts walls between people. Age does too. I try to mind my own business, which is a way of putting walls between me and others. The walls in my rooms find ways of separating one person from another, just as walls separate one room from another.

Walls have ears. The walls in my rooms have heard my secrets. I also associate walls with Wall Street, the most important money street in the United States, and money certainly does put distance between people. Walls are for pictures and colors and paper and sometimes even function as a canvas for an imaginative painter like a child. Of all these associations, the most intense one for me is the walls that people put up to separate one another.

Although walls provide me with privacy, they also provide me with distance in human relationships. I put up barriers to people very close to me so that they don't get too close. I can't help this in a way, because I need to survive just as you do. What kind of walls do I put up? I keep secrets from my family and from my friends. I don't ask a lot of personal questions of my friends, neighbors, and family, especially my children, because I want to make sure that they have their own lives and their own privacy. I don't have constant contact with people in my community just to make sure that we don't get bored with each other. I let others live their lives while I demand the freedom to live mine.

All these thoughts come to me while I am writing here, and I would want to use these thoughts in a speech about walls. For the beginning of my speech, I would probably say, "Builders put up walls to separate one room from another. But have you ever considered how you and I put up walls to separate ourselves from each other? Is it as necessary to put up walls between people in order to build your life as it is to put up walls in order to build your house? What kind of walls am I talking about?"

By this time, I would hope that my audience would be interested. Are you interested? If you are, complete the speech on your own.

Questions are as important for the middle of speeches as they are for the beginnings. However, questions for the middle of speeches are asked by the speaker when he is preparing his speech, not in the speech itself. To get material for the middle of a speech, you have to ask yourself many of the journalist's questions—who, what, where, when, why, and how. You have to dig out of yourself what you feel and know about your subject.

For my speech about walls, I would have to ask myself questions like these: What walls do I know? Where are they located? How do I know that walls exist between me and someone else? What examples do I have that would show that I have suffered or had pleasure because of the existence of walls? As a child, I did not have my own room, so I had no place to hide. My children, on the other hand, go to their individual rooms and enjoy their privacy. When did I discover that there were walls between me and other people? Was the experience painful or pleasant? How did I feel about having walls between me and other people? If I could, would I take a sledge hammer and knock down any walls that I know? Walls seem to make secrets. Is there anything right or wrong about secrets? Questions such as these will begin to prompt answers that will form the bulk of my speech on walls. They will lead me to a search for specific examples and genuine information about my life with walls, with walls I have known.

The ending of my speech about walls will begin with the statement of what I have told my audience. "I have let you in on my secret walls, and I wonder if you have ever thought about your own. By talking like this, I have shattered some of those walls, but I know that I have many more. In fact, I will probably replace the walls I knocked down with you today with new walls which I will construct tomorrow. Walls describe my house and they define my life. What secret walls are there in your life?"

I hope you have enough of a hint from what I've just said about how to begin a speech, find a middle, and choose an ending. Try it. Don't worry about the length of your speech. Worry about the value of it. You may want to return to the list from which I chose *Walls* to find a topic for your first formal speech. But you should feel free to add to that list.

Now that you're talking in front of your class (and I hope enjoying it), you may want to try another speech based on a list of one-liners I have collected for you. Choose one that interests you and see what you can do with it. Remember, you want to make a speech that has a beginning, a middle, and an end. Here's the list:

> The majority is always wrong.
> If you don't know where you're going, any road will take you there.
> What's good for General Motors is good for the U.S.A.
> It's a shame to waste youth on the young.
> The trouble with the morning is that it's so early.
> Education for all is education for none.
> Hell is other people.
> Hell is the inability to love.
> The man is strongest who most stands alone.
> That man is rich who has a scratch for every itch.
> Dreams are okay as long as they pay.
> The man who doesn't dream is like a man who doesn't sweat.

Now, I'd like to ask you to do two more activities before you finish this chapter. The first activity consists of a list of platitudes. In each pair, the second platitude contradicts the first. Choose one pair and make a short argument for one side, and then make one for the other side. Later in the book you'll be doing activities of a similar kind when you read about various forms of formal disagreement, such as discussion and debate. Use specifics to illustrate the points of your argument.

> Ignorance is bliss.
> 'Tis better to have loved and lost than never to have loved at all.
>
> Absence makes the heart grow fonder.
> Out of sight, out of mind.
>
> A penny saved is a penny earned.
> You can't take it with you.
>
> Look before you leap.
> He who hesitates is lost.

Too many cooks spoil the broth.
Many hands make light work.

Great minds think alike.
Fools seldom differ.

Think about the pair of platitudes you chose. Was it easier to argue one side than the other? If that was the case, did it have something to do with your own feelings about the statement?

Now, I'd like to ask you to read a short play I once wrote. The play is called "The Decent Thing." After you've read the play, I'd like to ask you to do some specific things with it, but there's no reason why you can't read it aloud in class, or act it out, even though we won't be talking about acting until later in the book. There are three characters in the play, two men and one woman. Neal Snyder is the mayor of Greenfield, a not very large town in a midwestern state. Right now he is receiving a deputation of two somewhat irritated citizens, Orvil Caldwell and Maude Cooper.

Orvil Caldwell: We've sent you the petition, Mayor, and we came to hear your answer.
Mayor Snyder: I know that, and I don't know what to say to you.
Maude Cooper: Does that mean that you haven't decided yet?
Mayor Snyder: Yes, I guess it does. I want to help.
Maude Cooper: The only way to help, Mayor Snyder, is for you to do your duty as mayor of Greenfield. You just go down to Michaels's Drugstore and tell Sam Michaels to get those dirty magazines off his shelves immediately.
Mayor Snyder: I know this is what you want me to say. I wish I could say it.
Orvil Caldwell: Just open your mouth, Mayor, and let the words come out. It's easy.
Mayor Snyder: It's not easy for a lawyer who's spent his entire career defending free speech and a free press.
Orvil Caldwell: You're not a lawyer now, Mr. Snyder. You're mayor.
Maude Cooper: You represent the people of Greenfield, Mayor Snyder. You're their spokesman. It's your duty to carry out the wishes

of this community. And this community wishes those pornographic magazines out of the hands of our young innocent children.

Mayor Snyder: Young they are, Mrs. Cooper, but innocent I'm not so sure.

Orvil Caldwell: But, Mayor, I would at least like to think they are innocent until proven guilty.

Maude Cooper: If anything would drive them to being guilty it is that smut in Sammy Michaels's store. You would never find me looking at that trash.

Mayor Snyder: You had to look at it, didn't you, to know that it was trash?

Maude Cooper: That was purely in line with my duty as a member of the Citizens for Decency.

Mayor Snyder: And what do you say, Mr. Caldwell, about that foul literature? You must have read it?

Orvil Caldwell: I can tell from the way you're acting, Mayor, that you're not in total agreement with Maude and me and the committee.

Maude Cooper: Not just us, the whole town.

Mayor Snyder: I know that you are speaking for the people of Greenfield.

Maude Cooper: And all the people of Greenfield, Mayor, expect you to speak for them. We all know you. We know that in your heart you can't approve of that kind of dirt.

Mayor Snyder: But whether or not I approve of it is not the question, Mrs. Cooper. The question is, Do I have the right to demand the removal of a magazine published and distributed for public purchase?

Maude Cooper: They don't purchase anything, those young ones. They just stand around and call their friends over to look. It's disgusting, absolutely disgusting.

Orvil Caldwell: It's bad, Mayor, and it's going to get worse before it gets better.

Maude Cooper: It won't get worse if people start behaving the way they should. If you want to help, there's one thing to do. Take the petition to Sam Michaels and shove it under his nose and say, "Get that filth out of here."

Mayor Snyder: If you were mayor, Mrs. Cooper, you would have no problem. But I'm quite different. I'm a lawyer—

Orvil Caldwell: A mayor.

Mayor Snyder: I am a lawyer who, as I told you, has devoted his entire career to trying to understand and practice the principles upon which this country was founded and continues to operate. I believe in free speech and a free press, and I would hope and pray that young people would develop good taste and a good sense of distinguishing between something worthwhile and trash.

Maude Cooper: Well now, you certainly must be enough of a lawyer to know about a clear and present danger, wouldn't you say?

Mayor Snyder: Yes, I do. I know the Supreme Court decision well.

Maude Cooper: And what does it mean? It means if people don't have the good sense to do the right thing for themselves, somebody has to do it for them. And that's exactly what we're doing here. We recognize a clear and present danger to the health and happiness of our children. I hope you don't begin to think you're more important than the people who have elected you.

Orvil Caldwell: Maude's right, Mayor Snyder. Now, mind you, we are not saying the people ain't behind you. You are without doubt the most popular mayor this town ever had, but nothing you did could be worth much if you don't get reelected, and the whole town, believe me, is expecting you to stand up to Sam Michaels.

Maude Cooper: Orvil is absolutely right, Mayor.

Mayor Snyder: Aren't you ever wrong, Mrs. Cooper?

Maude Cooper: Not this time, I'm not. We're speaking for Greenfield, and you've got to speak for us. When we went to Sam Michaels, he said, "The only time I will take those magazines off the rack is when Neal Snyder walks in here and tells me to."

Mayor Snyder: Mrs. Cooper, I don't want kids to read that junk, but I don't believe that one man has the right to determine what another person should be allowed to read.

Maude Cooper: Not one man. It's not just you, it's all of us. You are just the spokesman, but you have to do the job.

Orvil Caldwell: It's like you're the ball carrier and we are all your blockers. We can't make a touchdown unless you carry the ball across the line. You carry us across now, Mayor, and we will carry you across at election time.

Maude Cooper: Are you ready now to come down to Sam Michaels with us?

I would like you to answer Mrs. Cooper's question, pretending that you are Mayor Snyder. Tell her what your decision is, and explain why. This can become a short speech for you to make in class. Then, think back to the platitudes which I asked you to argue from both sides. I would like you to do the same here with Mayor Snyder's answer: after you've given your first answer to Mrs. Cooper, take the opposite point of view and again explain the reasons for your answer.

I would also like you to think about the persuasion of the two members of the committee, since persuasion is the subject of the next chapter in your book. What kinds of persuasion can you identify? Appeals to reason? Application of the law? Political threats? What else? I hope the next chapter will help you to see how some of these forms of persuasion work, and perhaps you'll want to look again at the play after you read about persuasion. In the meanwhile, good luck with your last speech in this chapter—your answers to the members of the committee.

Try a little tenderness.

Persuade your father to stop smoking.
Persuade your teacher to hold class outside under a tree.
Persuade your friend to share the expense of buying a motorcycle.
Persuade your parents to buy a new kind of cereal.
Persuade your friend to go on a hitchhiking trip.
Persuade your mother to let you go away for the weekend with some friends who are your age.
Persuade your father to give you a ride to a friend's house.

LOOK AT IT MY WAY

As you can see from the list of potential speeches that open this chapter, most of your life and mine is filled with instances of persuasive talking. We spend a great deal of time trying to persuade the people with whom we have daily contact to do what we want them to do: to help us in a moment of need, to provide us with what we want, to agree with us on a point of view. When persuasion is successful, you have convinced someone. To illustrate the difference between persuading someone and convincing that person, a teacher of mine once told me, "You may be persuaded of the value of the Red Cross by listening to one of its representatives tell you the merits of the organization; however, you won't prove you were convinced until you send them a check for ten dollars."

Civilized persuasion is a part of living since so much of our lives is devoted to influencing those around us, and in turn being influenced by them. Persuasion by force, on the other hand, is a less desirable form of persuasion, even contemptible on occasion, since it involves

Would you buy a used car from this man?

coercion by intimidation, bullying, brutality, and finally war. My concern in this chapter is primarily with civilized persuasion.

In civilized persuasion—a special form of communication—the listener is able to use his intelligence, his knowledge, and his wits in order to respond to the speaker. Ideally, the instruments of persuasion should be logic, reason, information, and common sense. But, because the speaker usually has a personal investment in trying to persuade his listener, he uses emotional appeal as well as reason.

What you are actually trying to do when you attempt to persuade someone is to get your own way. For example, I tried to persuade you to read this book in the opening chapter. I tried to find the most suitable style to encourage you to do what I want you to do, so I also made a record. I told you about myself, and spoke directly to you in hopes of persuading you to join my side. My record is, in a sense, a speech of persuasion. I used information, speculation, new material, sincerity, and, I hope, warmth. I not only tried to use reason, but I appealed to you emotionally. All persuasion has the emotional component to it because the speaker always has something at stake.

When a speaker has no real investment in what he is saying, the chances are that he will be less convincing. We talked about that earlier when I asked you to describe one of your happiest or saddest days. When you have a personal involvement, you will inevitably reflect that involvement. And sometimes that dimension becomes the crucial element in influencing your listener.

Some of us tend to be suspicious of the emotional aspects of persuasion, and for good reason. Demagogues like Hitler represent the extreme. But many advertising pitchmen, salesmen, and politicians illustrate why we should be suspicious of the emotional appeals of persuasion. Nevertheless, any speech attempting to persuade is certain to have an emotional element to it, and, rather than ignore it, it is wise for you to examine the value and nature of it.

Let's take the first suggestion in this chapter as an example of what I've been telling you. Persuade your father to stop smoking. You can collect all the evidence that will appeal to reason and logic: studies about the incidence of cancer, people you have known who have died of lung disease caused by smoking, doctors' reports, surveys, the Surgeon General's warning. You can marshall all this evidence and offer it to your father in a conversation, speech, or even a lecture in an attempt to influence him. However, if you add to that list an emotional appeal that you love him, that you know he cares enough about his family to give up that horrible and dangerous habit, that last appeal may have more influence than all the facts you can muster. And what's wrong with that? Certainly you have a right to convince him that loving you should inspire him to treat you well and that the best treatment would be to insure his good health as much as possible. Your appeal would be not only to his head, but also to his heart. It is the mixture of head and heart, reason and compassion, that persuades best.

I must tell you an instance of unsuccessful persuasion in my house recently. Dave came running home one day and asked his mother and me if we would let him buy a monkey. We immediately answered, "Not very likely." But he quickly argued, "But, they're on sale at the pet shop for only fifteen dollars this week. They regularly sell for ninety."

Have you ever tried to use arguments like that? Can you think of the last thing you tried to persuade somebody of? What appeals did you use? Did you try to bully? Reason? Intimidate? Excite? Flatter? Try to keep an account of one day's attempts at persuasion. You might be surprised at how often you try to influence the behavior of other people.

Much speechmaking is devoted to persuasion—that is, to persuading the listener to agree with the speaker's argument or to agree to act in a way that the speaker wishes. For example, in the next chapter you will read a political speech by Adlai Stevenson in which he used facts, intelligence, logic, irony, humor, and mockery as means of encouraging his listeners to vote for him in the 1952 presidential election. Politicians usually try to persuade, of course. But most of us do the same thing politicians do in our own ways. My wife tries to persuade me to take a vacation, and I try to persuade her to go to a play.

The assumption in persuasion is that the listener is somehow an adversary—that is, that he is opposed at the outset to the speaker's preference. The speaker then tries to change the listener's mind.

The most crucial thing to discover as an aid in encouraging another person to change his mind is to find out where your listener is vulnerable. Vulnerability is that part of a person's character which is capable of being touched or wounded. Children are often very clever at sensing vulnerability without really knowing it. We can make assumptions about vulnerabilities, often with very little evidence. Using your common sense, you know that you would try to influence a businessman by appealing to his sense of financial profit. You would influence a vain girl by appealing to her sense of flattery. You would appeal to parents' sense of the well-being of their children, just as you would appeal to a student with his report card, to a frugal man with his budget. The list is, again, so endless that you can make up your own. How do you appeal to your teachers? Your minister? Your neighbor? Your buddy? Your grocer? Members of your family?

The question of vulnerability is very important to understand, because the temptation to exploit another person's vulnerability, either for fun or for profit, is very great, even when you don't know what it is you are doing. It's even more dangerous when you do know what you are doing. It certainly works in my house. My children are always making appeals to my feelings—especially guilt. For example, if I am not home for a few days because my work requires traveling, they will ask me for favors when I return, with pleas like the following: "You haven't been home for three days and you won't even drive me over to Tom's house!" Or Josh will appeal to me to see his basketball game by saying, "You didn't see my last game. Why can't you at least see this one?" He knows how to get to me. They all do. You surely know how to get to your parents, too. You know where they are vulnerable, even if you've never really analyzed it for yourself. Try to analyze or explain it now. If you don't want to tell your classmates, at least tell yourself.

Unfortunately, exploitation of vulnerabilities (as compared to the mischief I was describing earlier) frequently can go over into coercion or force. Using words to work on someone's vulnerabilities may be more subtle than physical force, but it is often no less coercive. A lot of advertising, for example, is notorious for influencing us in a coercive way without our even knowing it. If you don't believe me, read Vance Packard's book *The Hidden Persuaders.* There you'll learn how we are unconsciously coerced into buying certain products and holding particular attitudes.

Likewise, most politicians are masters at exploiting the vulnerabilities of people they represent. At the present time, for example, the majority of people who live in cities are frightened about their safety. For that reason, many politicians have been seeking votes on a law-and-order platform. The city people are vulnerable to such an appeal, not necessarily because the candidate has revealed an intelligent plan or program to combat crime in the streets, but because the citizens fear crime. By promising security to voters, a politician endears himself to them and wins their votes. They may have no evidence that he can do anything about the crime problem, but they so greatly need to be reassured that they will have protection that they will cheer any candidate who vehemently argues in favor of a tough street policy. This appeal (which, incidentally, ignores some problems of justice while emphasizing the need for law and order) persuades a public threatened with crime in the streets to support the candidate who most loudly proclaims that he will bring safety.

Persuasion which appeals to fears rather than reason can make it easy to take advantage of people. Your parents may worry about someone taking advantage of you because they recognize your vulnerability. Or they may worry about your taking advantage of someone else because you know where that person is weak. The danger is not in the existence of vulnerabilities. We all have them. The danger is in the exploitation of them. Can you give a speech on one of these topics: Exploiting My Friends, I Am a Victim of Exploitation, Vulnerabilities I Have Noticed, or It'll Work Every Time?

It is possible that you will look upon being vulnerable as a weakness. After all, being vulnerable means that you can be subject to another person's will when you don't want to be. But rather than call being vulnerable a weakness, I would like to consider it a part of the human condition. It is a part of being open, and I would like to be able to be made to laugh or even cry by other people. Flattery will always get you somewhere because all of us have some vanity in us. It is part of my human nature and yours. When it gets too extreme, it can be dangerous. But, kept within some control, vanity and flattery reflect our humanness. We are by no means perfect, but that doesn't mean that anyone should exploit another person's imperfections, no matter how tempting. To be human is to be vulnerable. Just imagine how vulnerable you are with those whom you love.

As you have already discovered, some of us are suckers for certain kinds of appeals. I like originality, imagination, and resourcefulness. When someone exhibits those qualities around me, he is apt to get what he wants from me. I remember walking down Lexington Avenue in New York City a few years back and passing a number of panhandlers asking for handouts. After having lived in New York for some time, I had become rather callous about those people, especially when I realized that I was giving my nickles, dimes, and quarters for them to buy whiskey rather than food. I may have been overly self-righteous about the whole thing, but that was my attitude. Then another panhandler approached me and said, "Mister, I've got fifty-nine dollars and seventy-five cents saved up to see my dentist in Honolulu to have my teeth fixed. The ticket is sixty dollars. Could you give me the last quarter so I can make it?" Needless to say, I gave him my last quarter. How inventive are you when you are trying to persuade someone?

Necessity is said to be the mother of invention. If you need something badly, you are apt to invent more imaginatively than you will on those occasions when you can take it or leave it. That is why it is important to know just what is at stake when you make your appeal. The quality of your involvement may considerably influence the eloquence of your expression. Remember what Kurt Vonnegut, Jr., said about people speaking best when they are most passionate? Make an imaginative appeal to cancel classes today. Make an imaginative appeal to put off doing your homework. Make an imaginative appeal to remain up after you have been told to go to bed. Make an original appeal to rearrange the living room in your home. Invent ways to persuade a boy or girl you like to go out with you on Saturday night when you have already been told no. In making such an appeal, you'll probably agree that necessity is indeed the mother of invention.

I started this chapter by talking about civilized persuasion—a form of persuasion devoted to reason, logic, and intelligence. These qualities are to be encouraged in any persuasive speech. Although we may be able to lie with facts and figures, nothing can be so influential in a persuasive speech as facts and figures. If you want to convince me to give up driving a car and to take up bicycling, you can accomplish that objective best by citing the danger to my life and my family's lives— giving me facts and figures about pollution. If you want to persuade me of the danger of the population explosion, you should cite statistics that tell me of the danger of large numbers of people. Don't underestimate the power of figures, facts, information, and evidence.

Of course, I've already said that emotional appeal is a strong factor. And you know that evidence alone may not persuade. You have to learn how to use the evidence you accumulate. The real secret is bringing the evidence home to your listeners, making facts and figures mean something to them in their everyday lives. Color, eloquence, and passion in your speech of persuasion, together with the recognition of your listeners' vulnerabilities, make for a most effective and imaginative speech.

Some people try to persuade by yelling. I do this sometimes at home with my family, and sometimes it works—momentarily. More often than not, though, they let the shouting wear off and go on their own ways, ignoring what I have attempted to convince them of. Some people persuade by silence. Have you ever been in an argument with someone who remains silent? Have you ever been out on an occasion when your date says, "I want to go home," and you say, "I want to stay"? You make arguments to stay while your date remains perfectly silent. Eventually, you give up the fight and go home.

Can you recall the most recent instance of your having been persuaded of something you did not at first agree with or want to do? Was your disagreement or reluctance a matter of your principles? Better judgment? Common sense? Prejudices? Wishes? Dreams? Fears?

As you can readily see, persuasion is by no means of one kind only. Could you persuade your class, by the use of logic, to accept your position on one of the following?

>   Amnesty for Vietnam defectors.
>   The desirability of living in the city rather than in the country.
>   The desirability of living in the country rather than in the city.
>   Stronger penalties for heroin pushers.
>   Less free time for teachers.
>   The value of TV for young people.
>   The necessity of education for success.

I have asked you here to use logic in making your persuasive speech. That means you will want to be reasonable, although you may be witty. Now, take the same subject you chose and in another speech emphasize its emotional aspects to influence your classmates. For each of the subjects listed you must have some feelings. Examine those feelings, and, on the basis of your own convictions, try to change your audience's attitude, which you assume to be contrary to your own.

Now, as a final persuasive speech, blend your speech using logic with your speech using emotional appeal. This integration makes for an ideal speech of persuasion.

Let me say this about that.

Now that you've been making various kinds of speeches and thinking about persuasion, I will invite you to join me in looking closely at a political speech made by the late Adlai Stevenson. I would like to analyze with you some of the devices used in this speech. Some of them are ones you've been using in class. We will focus on several rhetorical devices—tricks of speechmaking—at the end of the chapter.

LOOK AT IT HIS WAY

Adlai Stevenson is regarded as one of the most significant and successful speechmakers in this century. His speeches have been collected in a number of volumes, and I would recommend that you go to a library or a bookstore and find one. He was the Democratic Party's nominee for President in 1952 and 1956 and Ambassador to the United Nations from January 1961 to July 1965. His speechmaking goes back long before 1952. In fact, one volume of his speeches on international affairs is a collection of speeches started in 1936. The speech you are about to read was made during his campaign in September of 1952 to an audience at Mosque Auditorium in Richmond, Virginia. The title of the speech is "The New South."

I was reminded that my grandfather, then a candidate for Vice President, spoke here in Richmond exactly sixty years ago this week in the old Academy of Music. According to the newspaper account, the audience responded "enthusiastically" to his "exposure of the iniquities of the Republican tariff system," and he took his seat amid "deafening applause."

Man is by nature a political animal.

For the deafening applause his grandson is prepared to await the conclusion of his remarks, and meanwhile any reference to Republican iniquities will be wholly unintentional!

Here in Richmond tonight, in Virginia, rich both in history and in the knowledge of its history, I am moved to talk for a few minutes of the past.

This is not an idle task. We can chart our future clearly and wisely only when we know the path which has led to the present. A great American philosopher has said that those who can't remember the past are condemned to live it again.

The South is a good place to take our bearings, because in no part of the country does the past—a past of great nobility and great tragedy—more sharply etch the present than in the South. It is a good place to think of the grim problems of war and peace which weigh so heavily on all of us today. For here we can best learn the lessons suggested by the peace of 1865, made when the great voice of moderation had been stilled. (I have been privileged to live for four years in Springfield, Illinois, the home of Abraham Lincoln.) The victor's settlement permitted the South to keep its charm, its mockingbirds, and its beaten biscuits. For himself the victor retained only the money and the power.

It took the South decades to recover. During these bleak years, from 1865 to 1912, the Republican Party was constantly in power, except for the two discontinuous terms of Grover Cleveland. In one of them my grandfather was privileged to serve as Vice President. And, again, between Woodrow Wilson and Franklin Roosevelt, the Republican Party had another long term of rule. The Democratic Party, therefore, had the dubious distinction of wandering in the desert for a longer time than the Children of Israel after their flight from Egypt.

For the South this period was a desert without an oasis. But, however hard it was to bear at the time, we in the more fortunate present can view it with a semblance of charity. For the Republican leadership did not neglect the South and other Democrats simply because you were Democrats. In its frozen impartiality it also neglected Republican farmers, small businessmen, and working people. Men earned the neglect of the Republican leaders not by their political affiliation, but by being small and poor. And this is why so many people have shifted to the Democratic Party.

The Republican leadership did not merely treat the South with arrogant and massive neglect. It did more. It shackled the South, and millions outside the South, through its control of Congress; its control of money and banking; its favoritism to powerful interests; its espousal of high tariffs, high interest rates and unfair freight rates.

In the larger sense you became colonials of an empire which, if it was not alien, was at least absentee. Yours was primarily an agricultural economy, depending for cash income largely on cotton and tobacco. Of these you produced far more than could be consumed at home.

You paid exorbitant rates of interest for mortgage and crop loans. Nobody consulted you about freight rates. You just paid them. Crops sold for what they would bring because farmers could not hold them for higher prices. Bitterly they witnessed prices rise only after their crops had gone out of their hands.

It is interesting to recall that more than half a century ago Southern and Western farmers pleaded for government warehouses where they could hold their crops for better prices to exchange for certificates at 80 per cent of the market value. The plan was denounced by Republican leaders as socialistic, a phrase they evidently never get tired of. But now, since the Democrats have enacted essentially the same plan, the Republicans approve enthusiastically. Indeed, bidding for the farm vote up in Minnesota the other day, the Republican candidate for President pulled the Democratic platform right out from under me!

But to return to the past. When you marketed your crops abroad, you sold in free markets for the going price. But when you bought manufactured goods at home, Republican tariffs compelled you to pay through the nose. You have been protesting this injustice since at least the year 1828.

Of course the Republican tariff wasn't all bad. It generously permitted Americans to worship at duty-free altars; eat from duty-free tin cans;

import duty-free yachts; be hanged with duty-free rope; and admire duty-free paintings in museums.

The Republicans were still at their old game only a little while ago, and I wish we could be sure they would not return to it if they have a chance. Over the protest of over a thousand American economists, they enacted the Smooth-Hawley tariff that raised rates to an all-time high. I need not tell Virginians, or your tobacco-growing and tobacco-processing neighbors, what that did to tobacco exports. Nor need I remind Southern cotton growers and cotton manufacturers how they were harmed; or say that this tariff was a turning point in precipitating the worldwide depression of the 1930's.

But I am not going to talk about the depression when the average yearly income of the families of one Southern state was $500. I have said—and I repeat—that I am not running against President Hoover. Indeed, I think all of us have reason to be grateful to him for the work of the Hoover Commission. And the fact of the matter is, I don't know who I am running against, but I strongly suspect that it is Senator Taft after all.

But I most certainly am running against the unchanging and apparently unchangeable attitudes of the Republican leadership. Presidents come and go. But attitudes remain. For a political party, as a man, is the sum total of its inheritance, environment, experience and attitudes.

Thus, for example, when the depression was coming on, the Secretary of the Treasury was Andrew Mellon. What was his formula for dealing with the depression? How did he propose to act when the magnificent promise of American life seemed at a shabby and ignominious end? Mr. Hoover, in his recently published memoirs, tells us. It was: "Liquidate labor, liquidate stocks, liquidate the farmers, liquidate real estate."

That is certainly one way to deal with a depression—the graveyard way. But somehow the American people were less than enthusiastic about it, and they turned to the Democratic Party which held out the prospect of life and hope.

The Democratic Party of today was born, then, of the sufferings of the people. It is neither all-wise nor all-knowing, for these are not man's gifts, but God's. But it is now—as it always has been—compassionate, merciful, humane; no stranger to human needs and wants and fears.

The task of striking off the shackles of the South, begun by Woodrow Wilson, has brought you to your rightful place in the Union, not as a matter of charity, not as a sectional matter, but because a happy, purposeful people in a strong, prosperous country is the democratic goal. The Southern states, too, it seems to me, have played a large part in liberating men's creative energies and reaching these goals.

Everywhere this liberation of man's powers during the Democratic decades has brilliantly succeeded, but nowhere has its success been more marked than in the South. Here has come the richest flowering of a great region our nation has witnessed. A new vitality and creative energy is apparent in every aspect of Southern culture, material, intellectual and spiritual. Your colleges are crowded. There is a keen interest in the arts.

Some years ago a famous American critic said that the South was the wasteland of the mind. Yet at that very moment, I am told, so many of your housewives had novels simmering with the soup—among them Gone with the Wind—that many husbands had to wait for supper. And men—in an effort perhaps to keep up with their women, among them your own Ellen Glasgow—were writing books and plays, too. So it was that the Nobel Prize for Literature came to the Mississippian, William Faulkner, a prize that he accepted in an exalted address, extolling the unconquerable spirit of man.

If this means much to the nation, it also, I am sure, means much to you. Your way has often been hard. Yet you have always held that civilization is something more than the bending of the resources of nature to the uses of man. Man cannot live without bread, but his spirit cannot live by bread alone.

In the course of this resurgence, I hope that it may be possible for us to keep all that was good of the Old South, while embracing all that is good of the New South. Technicians can make a country, but they alone cannot create a civilization. There are riches in your inheritance which are sometimes overlooked—riches which the rest of the nation could borrow with great profit. I believe it was Gladstone who said that no greater misfortune could befall a people than to break utterly with its past.

Among the most valuable heritages of the Old South is its political genius, which in many respects was far ahead of its time. Even today some of the finest products of Southern governmental thought are only beginning to win the general acceptance which they have so long deserved.

A classic example, it seems to me, is the Constitution of the Confederacy. Scholars of constitutional law have long recognized it as a sound and most thoughtful document. It contained some brilliant innovations, including the so-called item veto—authorizing the President to disapprove individual items in an appropriation bill, without having to veto the entire measure.

This inspiration of the Confederate statesmen has since been incorporated into the constitutions of about three-fourths of our states, including my own state of Illinois.

Is it too much to hope that our Federal Government may soon adopt this priceless invention of Southern statesmanship? I hope not, because it is a most useful tool. It has enabled me to veto more appropriations, involving more money, than any Governor in Illinois history. And, by the way, forty-six other states had higher state tax burdens than Illinois in relation to the income of their citizens last year.

In other fields, I am glad to note, the Southern talent for government has won the recognition which is its due. Many of your states are among the best governed in the land. Southern diplomats have earned wholehearted respect in Asia and Europe. In Congress Southern leaders once again give wise and distinguished service to the nation, especially in the all-important area of foreign affairs. I am proud to have one of them, Senator John Sparkman of Alabama, as my running mate. And I am also proud that other such leaders—each himself a candidate for the Presidency—have given me their support—Senator Kefauver of Tennessee, and my distant kinsman, Senator Richard Russell of Georgia.

Just as the governmental contributions of the South sometimes were not fully appreciated in the past, so too, I suspect, some of the problems of the South have not been fully understood elsewhere. One of these is the problem of minorities—a problem which I have had occasion to think about a good deal, since my own state also has minority groups.

One thing that I have learned is that minority tensions are always strongest under conditions of hardship. During the long years of Republican neglect and exploitation, many Southerners—white and Negro—have suffered even hunger, the most degrading of man's adversities. All the South, in one degree or another, was afflicted with a pathetic lack of medical services, poor housing, poor schooling, and a hundred other ills flowing from the same source of poverty.

The once low economic status of the South was productive of another —and even more melancholy—phenomenon. Many of the lamentable differences between Southern whites and Negroes, ascribed by insensitive observers to race prejudices, have arisen for other reasons. Here economically depressed whites and economically depressed Negroes often had to fight over already gnawed bones. Then there ensued that most pathetic of struggles: the struggle of the poor against the poor. It is a struggle that can easily become embittered, for hunger has no heart. But, happily, as the economic status of the South has risen, as the farms flourish and in the towns there are jobs for all at good wages, racial tensions have diminished.

In the broad field of minority rights, the Democratic Party has stated its position in its platform, a position to which I adhere. I should justly earn your contempt if I talked one way in the South and another way elsewhere. Certainly no intellectually dishonest Presidential candidate could, by an alchemy of election, be converted into an honest President. I shall not go anywhere with beguiling serpent words. To paraphrase the words of Senator John Sharp Williams of Mississippi, better to be a dog and bay the moon.

I should like to say a word about the broader aspects of minority rights.

First, I utterly reject the argument that we ought to grant all men their rights just because if we do not we shall give Soviet Russia a propaganda weapon. This concept is itself tainted with communist wiliness. It insultingly implies that were it not for the communists we would not do what is right. The answer to this argument is that we must do right for right's sake alone. I, for one, do not propose to adjust my ethics to the values of a bloodstained despotism, scornful of all that we hold dear.

Second, I reject as equally contemptible the reckless assertions that the South is a prison in which half the people are prisoners and the other half are wardens. I view with scorn those who hurl charges that the South—or any group of Americans—is wedded to wrong and incapable of right. For this itself is an expression of prejudice, compounded with hatred, a poisonous doctrine for which, I hope, there will never be room in our country.

So long as man remains a little lower than the angels, I suppose that human character will never free itself entirely from the blemish of prejudice, religious or racial. These are prejudices, unhappily, that tend to rise whenever the minority in question is large, running here against one group, and there against another. Some forget this, and, in talking of the South, forget that in the South the minority is high. Some forget, too, or don't know about strides the South has made in the past decade toward equal treatment.

But I do not attempt to justify the unjustifiable, whether it is anti-Negroism in one place, anti-Semitism in another—or for that matter, anti-Southernism in many places. And neither can I justify self-righteousness anywhere. Let none of us be smug on this score, for nowhere in the nation have we come to that state of harmonious amity between racial and religious groups to which we aspire.

The political abuse of the problem of discrimination in employment, the exploitation of racial aspirations on the one hand and racial prejudice on the other—all for votes—is both a dangerous thing and a revolting spectacle in our political life. It will always be better to reason together than to hurl recriminations at one another.

Our best lesson on reason and charity was read to us by Robert E. Lee. It was not the least of his great contributions to the spirit of America that, when he laid down his sword, he became president of a small college in Lexington—now the splendid Washington and Lee University. There he remained the rest of his life; unifying, not dividing; loving, not hating.

As the autumn of 1865 was coming on, General Lee, in one of the noblest of American utterances, said: "The war being at an end, the Southern states having laid down their arms, and the questions at issue between them and the Northern states having been decided, I believe it to be the duty of everyone to unite in the restoration of the country and the reestablishment of peace and harmony . . ." Later he said, "I know of no surer way of eliciting truth than by burying contention with the war."

We have great need of Lee's spirit in this hour of peril to our country, when voices of hatred and unreason arise again in our land. As free men we shall always, I hope, differ upon many things. But I also hope that we shall never be divided upon those concepts that are enshrined in our religious faith and the charters of our country's greatness.

No one could stand here in Richmond without reverence for those great Virginians—Washington, whose sturdy common sense was the mortar of our foundations, and Jefferson, that universal genius who, proclaiming the Rights of Man when few men had any rights anywhere, shook the earth and made this feeble country the hope of the oppressed everywhere. And so it is today after nearly two centuries.

Fortunately for us all, the Southern political genius still lives. It flamed not long ago in Woodrow Wilson. It burns steadily today among Southern members of Congress, and among many of the leaders of your states.

Good politics make good government. In this campaign, I shall not try to minimize the tasks which we confront. That we shall pass through these troubled times I am sure, not by grace alone, but by faith, intelligence and implacable determination.

> In my travels about the country of late in quest of your confidence I have felt that determination, that indomitable spirit. But nowhere more than here where I suspect it is as strong today as it was in the spring of 1865, when the Army of Northern Virginia returned to their homes. They found a wasteland of burned houses and barns, fences fallen and ditches caved in, weeds, and sorrow brooding over the fields.
>
> That was in April. But by June a crop was growing. The next year the crop was larger, and the next year it was still larger, and so, painfully and slowly, with no help except their hands and the benison of God, the South started on its long march from desolation to fruitfulness.
>
> This is part of your great heritage. And if I could speak for all Americans as I now do for myself, I would say that it also is part of the great heritage of America.

Here, in one speech, you can find nearly everything I've been talking about with you so far. I have specifically chosen a political speech that was delivered over two decades ago because I would like you to look objectively at the tactics of the speech, the appeals to reason and emotion, rather than bring your own political views to bear here. It might be interesting for you to make your own list of the changes that have come about since this speech was delivered. The struggle for minority rights was only smoldering at that time, the United States was at war in Korea, the fear of an internal communist takeover held the country in its grip, and the traditional political coalitions—the South and the Democratic Party, business and the Republican Party—had not begun to change into today's liberal and conservative coalitions.

The title of Stevenson's talk, "The New South," immediately makes his listeners curious: "What was the *Old* South?" Does Stevenson tell them? He not only tells them, but he begins as if he had known the question would be asked. What does he say about the Old South? He puts his audience in the spirit of the Old South by referring to a speech made in the same city sixty years earlier by, of all people, his own grandfather. Thus the speaker gives his audience of strangers the sense that he has a connection with them and implies that they have significant things in common. He as much as says, "I belong here because of my ancestry; I know you and your neighborhood, and I, therefore, must know something about your problems. You can trust me even though I come from Springfield, Illinois, instead of Richmond, Virginia."

Audiences like to be connected to their speaker, for it gives them a feeling that their world is recognized and respected. They are put into a receptive frame of mind as a result because the speaker has given them something familiar. Although in some situations familiarity may breed contempt, a speaker who can establish a familiarity with his audience will usually get its attention earlier and hold it longer.

Stevenson has prepared his audience for a response in his very first paragraph. What response is that? What is the value of the second paragraph? Does that paragraph say anything about the Old South, or, for that matter, the New South? Do you see a relationship between the second and fourth paragraphs? Do you sense a design in the speech? If so, can you describe that design? What does the fifth paragraph say about the Old South? What is the lesson to be learned from the peace of 1865? What was the settlement in the peace of 1865? What is Stevenson's attitude toward that peace? What attitude does he assume is in the minds and hearts of his listeners?

Read the first ten paragraphs aloud. Say those paragraphs as if you were giving the speech. How long did it take you? In a very few minutes, Stevenson has done the following with his audience:

1. Established his identity with them through his grandfather.
2. Established the superiority of the Democrats over the Republicans.
3. Established his sense of humor as sophisticated and ironic.
4. Established that he is profound without being superior or intellectually elite.
5. Defined the spirit of the Old South.
6. Criticized the treatment of the Old South by the government.
7. Established his alliance with the audience.
8. Created a series of contrasts which will be the basis for his persuasion of the audience.

Can you explain, by citing particular sentences, how Stevenson has accomplished each of these? I think I have given you sufficient clues to help. Read carefully, and I think you'll find specific examples to justify each of my eight conclusions.

In the seventh paragraph, by citing specific examples, Stevenson distinguishes the role of the Republican Party from that of his own. By establishing that both his party and the Old South were victims of the Republican policies, he continues to emphasize his kinship with the audience. Stevenson encourages that kinship. He chooses pronouns—we, you—to foster the alliance. He explains the desert that his audience knows. What is he telling the audience that it wants to hear?

Stevenson has facts and figures to describe the Old South, the South of agricultural economy, the rural South. By looking upon the people in the audience as victims of Republican policies, he has their sympathy. Any audience likes someone in its corner, someone who believes it has been mistreated.

For a moment, let's look at the style of Stevenson's rhetoric. In the thirteenth paragraph, he speaks sarcastically, suggesting that the Republican Party has been helping the rich get richer, all the time realizing that his audience is made up of a poorer population. Explain how his sarcasm works. Would it work as well with you as it may have worked in Richmond?

In the fifteenth paragraph, Stevenson starts out saying, "I am not going to talk about the depression" (the result, an audience assumes, of Republican administration from 1920–29); yet he manages to get in that little statement, "when the average yearly income of the families in one Southern state was $500." That packs a huge wallop. By contrast ("I won't talk about it," followed by the very talking), he makes his point and at the same time maintains his posture of not being one to hit an opponent when the opponent is down. Stevenson maintains his civilized, humble, honorable posture while at the same time he is strongly criticizing the Republican administrations since 1865, painting a picture of a party which punished the South and exercised unjust policies. He leaves his audience believing that their only friend is the Democratic candidate. He presents himself as a gentleman.

In the meantime, the audience is waiting to hear about the New South and how Stevenson will help them. And Stevenson's timing is perfect: without saying so directly, he tells the audience that the Democratic Party is God's associate. The party he describes has the same qualities he associates with God—compassion, mercy, humanity. He has prepared his audience for this association with a slight reference in the sixth paragraph that compares the people of the Old South to the Children of Israel. Stevenson knows that his audience is made up of God-fearing people, average people, humble people, needy people. His speech touches them where they live. His language is their language, his facts are clear, his implications are gentlemanly (unless you go below the surface).

Now Stevenson moves from the Old South to the beginnings of the New South. He doesn't say what the New South is. Instead of telling his audience that the New South is becoming industrial and therefore wealthier than the old agricultural South, he says that colleges are flowering and that there is a keen interest in the arts. Certainly his southern listeners must have been flattered by the praise of *Gone with the Wind,* Ellen Glasgow, and William Faulkner—perhaps so much so that they forgot to think that the New South was considerably more different from the Old South than Stevenson says. Stevenson wants his audience to believe that their economic status is improved because the Democratic Party has taken care of the farmer, not because the farmer has become a factory owner.

How well does Stevenson seem to know his audience? In the first part of his speech he talks about bread (economy), and then he says, "Man cannot live by bread alone." He flatters the audience with the contributions to the nation of southern artists, culture, and statesmen. Have these contributions been made possible by the Democratic Party and its principles? Is the New South factually better off economically than the Old South? Is the plight of the blacks different in the New South? How does Stevenson address himself to the question of minority rights? Do you think it would be fair to say that he takes such a large view of that subject that it amounts to no position at all?

A political speech such as the one delivered by Adlai Stevenson is designed to influence an audience. It is a speech of persuasion, and it employs all the tactics you read about in the last chapter. There is nothing dishonest in Stevenson's speech, although you can certainly find instances when Stevenson raises a question such as minority rights and leaves it unanswered. The goal of a political speech is to persuade everyone in an audience to vote for the candidate, to offend no one. Therefore, Stevenson is careful to hold out the question of minority rights and then conceal it with an immediate reference to communism—something he can be sure everyone in his audience is opposed to. His speech directs itself to all of the people in the audience so he balances every stand he takes, as all political speakers do. He is cautious, and he offends no one. Therefore, he has to choose rhetoric and organization for his speech that will give the appearance of a man of strength and conviction while at the same time saying nothing that can be held against him. Look carefully at the last quarter of the speech. In practically alternating paragraphs, Stevenson assures his audience of his integrity, yet makes no specific pledges. Perhaps that's better than saying nothing, but, when it comes to specifics, nothing may be just what he is saying—in a most eloquent fashion.

I disapprove of what you say

> Here's to you, and here's to me,
> And if by chance we disagree,
> To heck with you,
> And here's to me.

That poem—a drinking toast—may sound too harsh, arrogant, or egocentric to you. But in the final analysis, tolerating another's opinion about anything is not an easy task, and sometimes it is even impossible. We claim that we tolerate others' opinions. Sometimes we even claim that we agree with those opinions. But when we disagree, it is not likely we will be persuaded to change our minds unless something very dramatic is done. For that reason alone, we shoud try to examine and understand the nature of disagreement.

LET'S AGREE TO DISAGREE

but I will defend to the death your right to say it.

William Faulkner said that the subject of literature was "the heart in conflict with itself." Does Faulkner's statement make sense to you? Does your heart ever disagree with itself? Could you give a talk on the subject "My Heart Disagreed with Itself"?

If you and I have natural disagreement inside ourselves, imagine how easy it is to have disagreement with another person. Do you agree? Let's get down to specifics. Do you know the kind of inner conflict I'm describing? My heart disagrees with itself frequently in my attitudes toward my children, my wife, and my friends. I have a friend whom I find attractive and agreeable, but whom I also find a little phony. The disagreement in my heart is not very significant. But, nevertheless, I know that I have both happy and unhappy feelings about that friend.

Other examples: Tonight I want to do some work on this book, and I want to play bridge. Two young people may be caught between the desire to marry and the desire not to go through with it. You must know something of these conflicting feelings, which are really disagreements. However, you may not be likely to think of internal conflict as disagreement, because we usually associate the word *disagreement* with a difference of opinion between two people. But even with your own opinions, you may have disagreement. It is in those cases that your mind is in disagreement with itself, your heart in conflict with itself, or your mind and your heart at odds.

I am suggesting to you that disagreement is natural, necessary, and perhaps even desirable. Most of all, disagreement is not to be feared as much as it is to be nurtured. I feel the need to begin this chapter on formal forms of disagreement such as discussion and debate with what I have just said to you because I find so many people afraid of disagreeing in any way. I don't know if I have been seeing only the wrong people, but many of my students are very reluctant to disagree with me. My children are sometimes very careful about disagreeing with me, or arguing with me. My friends are too discreet to debate with me. I attribute all of this to their fear of being rejected. It goes under the guise of being afraid to hurt *me,* but, in reality, those people who believe they are afraid to hurt me are really afraid that if they disagree with me they will hurt themselves because I will not like them. They are afraid I will reject them, that I will withdraw my love or affection from them.

Do you know that feeling? Can you describe it from some experiences with your parents? What would you describe? Do you think we are afraid to disagree because we don't know how to disagree? Because we like harmony? Because we don't want to hurt other people?

Just as communication is not necessarily agreement, disagreement is not necessarily a failure to communicate. Nor is it true that people are so insecure and frightened that they cannot tolerate disagreement from others. It *is* true that just because you disagree you aren't necessarily right. I am simply posing the proposition that disagreement is natural and good, and I would like to think that you and I can agree to disagree.

To disagree is not to admonish, dismiss, dislike, or reject. It is to recognize a difference of opinion on something that neither you nor I have sufficient evidence to agree upon. The more evidence we get, the closer to agreement we may find ourselves. In the meantime, we talk about the things upon which we disagree, not necessarily to end up agreeing, but to find out what we can tell each other about our reasons for holding particular convictions or opinions. A disagreeable person is an unpleasant one, but a person who disagrees is frequently challenging, exciting, and lively.

Obviously, there are varieties of disagreement. Some people want to disagree just because they feel negative about a person or an idea. Some people like to bicker. My children drive me up a wall with their infernal bickering about everything—salt at the table, the light in the room, the radio, the TV. You probably know as much about this kind of disagreement as I do. Some people, on the other hand, like to disagree in order to encourage discussion.

Discussion is a civilized idea. It is usually contrasted with, rather than compared to, arguing. (Do you know the difference between *contrasting* and *comparing*? The distinction between the two words is important.) Discussion carries with it the connotations of controlled voices (rather than screaming), open minds, mutual respect, intelligence, and tolerance. Discussion does not usually imply the persuading of one person to agree with another. Discussion, in fact, brings to my mind the idea of two parallel lines never meeting, simply extending.

Arguing, on the other hand, implies raised voices, anger, a desire to force agreement, and intense persuasion. Do I speak from the same frame of reference as you do? Do you find that an argument is a situation in which one person tries desperately to convince another person of the correctness of his point of view?

Argumentation is carrying discussion into the realm of persuasion, and persuasion—as you read earlier—has many forms. When you discuss, are you really arguing? Can you speak on the level of disagreement without trying to persuade another person of the rightness of your opinion? Is it possible for you to discuss an issue without the discussion moving into an argument?

If you have been following me in these last few pages, you have been able to see the subtle shadings of disagreement, the number of ways in which we disagree with ourselves and with others. The shades of difference between bickering, discussing, arguing, and debating make disagreement a very vast subject indeed, and something for all of us to give some thought to. We all like harmony. We all know discord. To live with the coexistence of both conditions is our fate.

Many people believe that they can find harmony by agreeing with those around them. I, on the other hand, believe whatever harmony there is in life comes from the knowledge of discord. I say that about married couples, friends, parents and children, teachers and students, ministers and their congregations, government and the people.

I believe it is ultimately more preferable to battle with words than with guns. We are going to disagree and to argue, and even to fight. I favor fighting with words rather than with bullets. Sticks and stones will break my bones, but words will also hurt me. However, it is better to be wounded by words than destroyed by guns. That statement is a principle I hold in life, and one with which I write this book.

It is quite possible in my understanding of things that through bickering, discussing, arguing, and debating we may eventually find ourselves fighting. That the final fight should be in words, however, is my dream. I believe that with respect to my own life, that of my neighbors, friends, community, and, ultimately, my nation. Coexistence is the agreement to disagree. War is the demand to agree.

Informal means of disagreement are legion in your lives: conversations in classrooms, at dinner tables, in living rooms, on dance floors or football fields—in all these places, we may disagree. As informal disagreement changes into a more formal situation, the disagreement between people also gets more formal, culminating in the formal debate which is perhaps the most sophisticated and structured kind of disagreement. The irony in debate, which I will be discussing with you later in this chapter, is that two people or two teams express their disagreement on the subject for debate, but they might not really disagree in their minds and hearts. They choose to disagree, even to take positions opposite their own, in an intellectual exercise. In this challenge, they may have a personal investment or conviction, but they also may not. Accepting such a challenge is not easy for many of us. We frequently are not confident enough to meet the debating test. On the other hand, because it is an intellectual exercise, debate can help you to create and organize an argument that is reasonable and sound.

You may prefer informal discussion to more formal forms of discussion such as panels, forums, and symposiums, but I suggest that you expose yourself to the challenge of some form of argumentation. If nothing else, arguing with someone can often make you feel better. More formal kinds of discussion—committee discussions, panels, forums, symposiums, debate—are governed by rules which I will explain to you before you look at them. But first, I'd like to say something general to you about rules—and foul lines.

I first realized that foul lines meant the same thing to me as rules when I went to play baseball with my son Davie, who was six at the time. When we found a likely spot to play, I started to put down foul lines, and he resisted. "Come on, Daddy, let's play baseball!" I answered him, saying, "If you want to play baseball, you must have foul lines: to the left of one line is foul, and to the right of the other line is foul. Now, if you just want to hit a ball so that it doesn't matter where the ball goes, then I'll play that game with you. But that's not baseball."

Foul lines take the act of hitting a ball, remove it from chaos, and give it some order. They require the players to be more skillful. A baseball player must develop his skill at hitting a ball within the restrictions of the playing field. My son became a better baseball player as a result of the restrictions imposed upon him by foul lines.

I would like you to develop into a better speaker, and the foul lines imposed upon you by time, situation, facts, truth, and skill all help you to become a more effective speaker. Look around you, and notice the best speakers you've heard. Most of us do not speak well because we have no limits placed upon us. In fact, we avoid limits. But formal speaking has all kinds of foul lines, and knowing them can only help you to communicate better in any kind of talking or listening situation. Foul lines are changeable, just like emotions or fashion. The way you speak at the dinner table at home may not be the way you speak at the lunch table in your school cafeteria. You speak under two different sets of *unspoken* rules.

Foul lines for discussion groups such as committees, panels, forums, and symposiums usually involve the following:

1. The meeting is organized.
2. A chairman or moderator maintains order and fairness.
3. Preparation is required on the part of all the participants.
4. A decision should be reached by the end of the discussion.

These foul lines are by no means rigid, but they attempt to shape conversation into an organized activity that will help people to reach agreement or to become better informed. Not all of the discussion groups I've named must reach a decision that involves a vote or a recommendation, but all of them should permit you, either as a participant or as a listener, to better understand the topic under discussion.

All of you have no doubt served on committees to plan school activities. Committees usually are small groups which hold discussions so that they may either report their decisions to a larger group or work together on a project in an orderly way. For example, you might be asked to be a member of a committee to report to the student council on the need for additional locker space or a new grading system or a new elective program. You might also be a member of a committee assigned to decorate the school assembly room for a holiday party. Although your participation in the second kind of committee is essentially going to mean that you will be purchasing materials, making decorations, and putting them up, you will also first discuss, in an orderly fashion, what you are going to do and the best way of doing it. For that reason, the committee will probably have a chairman who will attempt to resolve any differences of opinion in your discussions so that your work will not be haphazard.

Discussion groups might be described as formal committees. The members of the group appear before an audience to discuss a specific topic, and each member of the group becomes a specialist on the topic so the discussion may be meaningful and informative for its listeners. A *panel discussion* is a discussion before an audience on a specific topic by a group of selected speakers. It is usually a small group which deals with a single problem. A *forum* is an assembly for the discussion of public affairs. Many TV shows are arranged in this way, particularly the shows you may watch at the end of each year when a group of newsmen review the closing year and make predictions about the next year. In a *symposium,* formal speeches on a particular subject are offered. The members of a symposium often discuss a topic of interest in one field of study—for example, a group of scientists might assemble to discuss new research on cancer before an audience.

I would suggest that with some classmates you participate in one of the discussion groups I've described to you, and make a presentation before your classmates. The nature of your material may help you to decide whether you wish to participate in a panel discussion, a forum, or a symposium. You may wish to choose one of the following topics for your discussion, or you may add to the list.

>   Choosing your own courses
>   Choosing your own teachers
>   Urban renewal
>   Rural renewal
>   Ecology in your community
>   The meaning behind today's headline
>   Your city government
>   The genetic code
>   Nonverbal communication
>   The new sound of radio
>   The school dress code
>   The value of a speech course
>   The novels of Kurt Vonnegut, Jr.
>   Choosing a college

Remember the general foul lines I've given you. For each discussion group, you will want to choose a chairman or moderator to obtain information on your subject, and to prepare your presentation. In the most orderly discussion groups, much work is done in advance so that the presentation may be informative and interesting to your audience. You may also want to invite questions from the audience and to take turns answering them.

Debate is the highest form of organized persuasion and orderly discussion. Debate is a means of dealing with a controversial issue in such a way that speakers for and against the proposition have equal time to state their cases. In traditional debate, two teams of two members each make the presentations, each person speaking twice. An affirmative team defends and argues for the proposition, while the negative team opposes it. The burden of proof is on the affirmative team, and research is of great importance. Because the affirmative team has the burden of proof, it has the privilege of making the first and last presentations. The first speeches are *constructive* speeches, during which both affirmative and negative present their cases for or against the proposition. The second speeches are *rebuttal* speeches, in which the statements of the opposing team are challenged and questioned. The structure of a formal debate looks like this:

First affirmative constructive speech
First negative constructive speech
Second affirmative constructive speech
Second negative constructive speech
First negative rebuttal speech
First affirmative rebuttal speech
Second negative rebuttal speech
Second affirmative rebuttal speech

Usually ten minutes is given for each constructive speech, and five minutes for each rebuttal speech. A timekeeper warns the speaker when time is running out, and the speaker is not allowed to speak past the allotted time.

Probably your state has contests each year so that debating teams from one school may match wits with teams from other schools. The traditional style of debate may be used, or the state may have its own style. I know of several states which hold meetings for debate using styles other than the one I have described to you. These debates are usually called *cross-examination* debates, and the organization of the debate varies from state to state. Your teacher can describe the method used in your state, or you may find out by making inquiry to the state forensic association.

Generally, one topic for debate is given for the school year, and the same topic is debated throughout the nation. Assume that the national debate topic is *Resolved: The United States should have a volunteer army.* As a debater, you will begin to prepare *both* affirmative and negative stands on the topic, after doing some research. When you have accumulated sufficient data, you will probably want to make an outline for your affirmative and negative positions, since you will argue both sides in contests. Your outline might look something like this:

Resolved: The United States should have a volunteer army

Affirmative: 1. A volunteer army is a motivated army with a positive attitude toward military service.
2. A volunteer army is professional in nature; therefore, it is more skilled and better organized.
3. A volunteer army is efficient and prepared (compared, for example, with the lack of preparedness for Pearl Harbor).
4. A volunteer army would not have so many defectors: the number of defectors from the draft army has been rising steadily since the Korean War.

Negative: 1. A volunteer army raises the danger of a powerful military force controlling the country. (Remember Eisenhower's warning about the military-industrial complex.)
2. The purpose of a professional army is to fight; the purpose of any profession is to practice its profession.
3. Nations which have professional armies have suffered abundant takeovers by inside forces.
4. A volunteer army could make citizens passive or apathetic; they may feel that they are protected but that they have little say in making democratic decisions.

You would obviously add to this outline as your research progressed. The more impressive your argument, the more likely your victory would be. And making an impressive argument involves building your case to its most intense and effective point, and then defending that case. For that reason, a debate is usually arranged with a strong opening statement to arrest attention, meaningful arguments in the middle, and a strong point to close the presentation.

The organization you must follow in debating is formal. But the organization you use in making your presentation comes from common sense and originality. You persuade your audience by the quality of your argument and the genuineness of your position. The more persuasive you can be about the intelligence of your argument, the better chance you have to influence others. The more real you make your case, the more effect you'll have upon your listeners. Conventional gestures and organization, abstract and general arguments, orthodox presentation may gain you some points. However, it is originality which convinces, examples which really illustrate, statistics which illuminate.

The following excerpt from a debate at the Cambridge Union in England may give you an idea of how wit and intelligence may be used to debate an issue. In England, heckling and applause from the audience is allowed, and the style is different from that used in the United States. The main speakers in this debate, held in 1973, were Germaine Greer, author of *The Female Eunuch,* and William F. Buckley, Jr., editor of the *National Review.*

PRESIDENT of the Cambridge Union: Good evening, and welcome, ladies and gentlemen. The motion before us is: "This House supports the Women's Liberation Movement." Guest speakers are Dr. Germaine Greer, who will be speaking in favor of the motion (laughter) and William F. Buckley, Jr., who will be speaking against (applause).

GERMAINE GREER: I ought now to say either "ladies and gentlemen," or "men and women." It strikes me as very odd that when I use the less ceremonial form of approach, I have to put the men first (laughter), and when I affect to belong to a class of ladies and gentlemen, I put the ladies first. It must be that one class is more skilled in hypocrisy than the other.

When I argue here for your support for the Women's Liberation Movement, I am asking you really to consider whether or not you can countenance the nonliberation of any group in your community, and whether or not you are so afraid of the characteristics and personalities of one-half of the human race that you cannot allow them room to move or a voice to be heard (applause).

I believe that at last men are beginning to realize where their own self-interest is best served. If you want better relationships with women (laughter), you are going to have to conduct yourselves in such a way that those relationships are possible.

Now when I talk about sexual tension, and dishonesty, and ignorance about the relationships between men and women in this university, I detect, arrogantly or not, a movement of sympathy. I think most people feel that this university in some ways enshrines the most incapacitating mistakes about the relationships between men and women in its attitudes toward each other. The fact that you are all here, in such numbers, is much more an indication, it seems to me, of—exactly what I was going to say—of what I call a "groupie" syndrome. The issue is not what interests you, because you are involved with peripheral issues, like how are these famous media performers going to handle themselves. Now I am sorry to disappoint you but I am not interested in delighting you with a song-and-dance routine with William Buckley (laughter) for whom I have rather more respect than you would be prepared to allow. I regard him as a man of intellectual probity, and part of my problem now is that I cannot understand altogether why Mr. Buckley is on the other side of the hall.

Women's Liberation has always been historically a minority movement; something which again is not repugnant to Mr. Buckley, who is himself in favor, it seems to me, of minority movements of one sort or another. It strikes me as very strange that whereas Tennyson could support most of Mr. Buckley's propositions about free trade, and the private sector, and private enterprise, Tennyson found no difficulty also in lending intellectual support to the idea of Women's Liberation. And Mr. Buckley, whose general political attitudes are about of the same vintage as Tennyson's, apparently finds it impossible to follow him.

I would have thought that everybody here, regardless of their sex, his sex—I beg your pardon; I would have thought that everybody here is aware that relationships between people who have full responsibility for their actions, full pride and security in what they do, a full readiness to stand by their intellectual pronouncements and their own morality—that relations like these are the only ones worth having. You must be tired of a situation of mutual exploitation and mutual dishonesty.

When we talk about the Women's Liberation Movement, we are talking about an impetus arising from the whole of our society, an impetus as old as our culture, which is at last moving into an area in which it can realize its most noble aspirations. Because it is now possible to control birth without risking life and destroying morality, because it is now possible to reorganize our industrial structures away from the importance of physical strength and toward the importance of dexterity, and application and goodwill; because these things are possible, it is now possible for the heartfelt cry of women who are not my grandmother or my great-grandmother, women whose lives were extinguished long ago, it is now possible for what they argued for to be realized. If it is realized, the result must be a better life for us all.

I don't mean more comfortable, because God knows for the first few generations it won't be. Because we have an enormous intellectual weight upon our shoulders. We have to invent a way of life which was never before possible. But at least we can argue in the true sense of "better" that we have a more moral existence when women act out of free choice, when they contract themselves to people out of free choice, when they produce work which is their best, when they are able to face criticism, when they have enough intellectual and spiritual muscle not to break down and be hidden by uxorious husbands from the pressure of cultural examination.

I am not talking to this audience as I would talk to those of my sisters who are working in factories, which it seems to be thought would be an innovation. One in three married women in this country are at work, and most of them in menial occupations. One in three married women in this most wonderful of all worlds.

(Dr. Greer sat down to a long ovation.)

WILLIAM F. BUCKLEY, JR.: I am of course here as an advocate, as is Miss Greer, whose brilliance is perhaps the principal asset of her movement. However, I do hope you will understand if I say quite bluntly that I would not have wasted your time, or spent a great deal of my own, if my burden here tonight was to oppose for women the "room to move," to quote Miss Greer, a "voice to be heard," to quote again Miss Greer. I do not remember ever having opposed educational opportunities for women, or for that matter industrial or political opportunities for women, and Miss Greer is quite correct in her insight that it is inconsistent with my general position to do anything of the sort.

We are here to debate not women's liberation, but the Women's Liberation Movement. Those who do not allow an important distinction between the two terms do not, for instance, allow a distinction between a fight against poverty and a movement against poverty that is led by representatives of an ideological creed. It is quite true that we might — you and I and Miss Greer — disagree on certain definitions of liberation itself, leaving the movement aside for the moment. Has in fact the sexual revolution given us the kind of liberation we exactly anticipated?

One of Miss Greer's especial charms is her willingness to communicate the whole gamut of her emotions to her followers, and also the whole gamut of her vocabulary (laughter). She was asked recently: "Do you fall in and out of love a lot?" and she replied, "I think I gave up falling in love when I was about nineteen. Since then I have allowed myself to be misled into it again. When that happens I become absolutely abject, utterly unscrupulous, totally dishonest, and I can do nothing about it. From being an interesting and independent woman, I just become a complete pain." I regret very much that Miss Greer is out of love (laughter).

But Miss Greer moves on on the assumption that the enslavement of women is something that can only be dislodged by revolutionary means. It does not do at all to suggest to her that in fact progress has been made, because she says that that progress is largely illusory. She told you here tonight she does not really believe that significant progress can be made because in fact women are locked into a relationship with men who are themselves the slave masters, who must themselves be liberated. It is impossible, she points out aphoristically, to liberate slaves without liberating the slave masters, and under the circumstances she says that we must have nothing less than revolution.

Tonight she talks occasionally and rather wincingly about some of the excesses of the movement. I gather that the excesses of the movement are tactically embarrassing to her at this moment, but the excesses of the movement are very definitely encouraged in her writings. She does not favor, for instance, excessive, or even discernible penalties for rape. Do you favor the tough penalties we now have for rape? Answer: "Absolutely not. I regard imprisonment as an inappropriate punishment for any crime." She talks here about a curious word. Did you notice that she uses the word contract between the woman and the man, a contract freely given. Heaven knows we all agree that any contract should be freely given, but the use of the word contract seems to be recidivist.

Again I say, what are our differences? My understanding of the movement is based on the writings of Miss Greer who, I repeat, says: We've got to have revolution, and we've got to upset all of the norms by which we have been bound. We have got to upset the notion of the family as the basic "nuclear," as she calls it, unit. We must have communes.

We must do away with religion. We must do away with family. There is something of that comprehensive concern of the worldmaker who says: "Because I do not choose to marry, people ought not to marry. Because I do not choose to rear a family, people ought not to rear a family." It is in the name of that that we are being invited to consider a movement toward the liberation of women, in the sense of giving them rights to which, I think, most people feel they are obviously entitled.

This, ladies and gentlemen, is the fundamental issue before the House. Can we divorce women's liberation from the Women's Liberation Movement? I say yes. Indeed we can. Can we assume that organic progress can be made in your society—and in mine—without revolution? Yes, I do believe that it can. Do we in fact feel that the time has come to transform society convulsively? Mr. Stephen Leacock remarked twenty-five years ago that the original college woman was a witch "with her incantations and prophecies, and the glow of her bright imagination; and if brutal men of duller brain had not burnt it out of her, she would be incanting still." It is not my proposal to burn the imagination or the enthusiasm of Miss Greer out of her, but it is my responsibility to resist some of the implications that she has grafted on, I think without license, to the Women's Liberation Movement.

(Germaine Greer was declared the winner as the motion passed 546–156.)

Charm me with language.

When you speak, you get considerable help from your body and your voice. You can use gestures such as pointing, raising your eyebrows, or shrugging. You can move about, waving your arms or shuffling your feet. And you can raise and lower your voice from shouts to whispers. In this way you not only say words, but you also carry the meaning of the words. When writers put words on paper, they have no such advantages. They have only the precision of their language and the aid of punctuation. For that reason, a writer tries to be concise, clear, and economical in using words. All writers are economical, but the poet is the most economical of all.

SAY IT WITH FEELING

Before I continue with this subject, I want to ask you a question: Have you ever had the experience of taking an essay test when you could give the answer in a paragraph or less because you knew exactly what you wanted to say? And have you had the opposite experience when you didn't know the answer, yet it took you a whole page to say so? Good writers, like good speakers, know what they are talking about and therefore should be able to say what they want to in the fewest possible words.

In my conversation with Kurt Vonnegut, Jr., which you read earlier, he said the following about economy in language:

> You should understand that I was trained in the use of language by managers of an industry which no longer exists, the short story

Words are nets to catch beauty by.

industry. The managers of this industry had certain rules about language in stories which I had to learn. These managers, these editors, required that whenever a character spoke in a story, what he said had to either advance the story or reveal something significant about the character. The demand was for efficiency. I learned that lesson so well and it is so automatic with me now when I write that when a character speaks he either advances the story or reveals something significant about himself, or he does not speak. This makes for efficiency; I don't know whether it makes for art. Anybody who follows those rules will write a story which moves faster, which is more exciting to the reader.

Vonnegut was talking about efficiency in language in the same way I am talking about economy in language. Does he use unnecessary words? Would you say he needs both phrases in the third sentence: "These managers, these editors"? Can you make a convincing case for the need for both phrases? For only one phrase? Can you make a similar case for the last two clauses, ". . . which moves faster, which is more exciting to the reader"?

When we speak, we frequently don't worry about being economical. In fact, we usually take the license that says, "If we are not boring, we can talk any way we want to." Sometimes we can get away with verbose talk in conversation, and sometimes we can't.

Good writers usually try to be spare and exact in their use of language, precisely because they don't have all the visual aids available to a speaker. That is why when you read a writer's words aloud, you must do so in a very careful way. The writer wrote the words to be read, not necessarily to be spoken. When you read silently to yourself, you can mull over words, reread lines, go back and see what was written before, scrutinize a sentence—all methods by which to read more accurately. You have time to discover the writer's meaning.

However, when you speak a writer's words aloud, your audience does not have the luxury of time, and they must hear the writer's meaning on your first reading. Such a situation, therefore, demands that the speaker of a writer's words take pains to understand what the writer is really saying.

When you take words off a printed page and begin to put them on a stage of any sort—a theater, a classroom, a street corner, a living room, or a kitchen—you must be sure to interpret the meaning of the author's language. You do this interpreting by emphasizing particular words, by pausing in certain places, by phrasing, by gesturing, and by manipulating your voice. These techniques have an influence on the sound of the author's words, sometimes resulting in vast distortion, sometimes misunderstanding, but sometimes in a more successful communication than the author may ever have dreamed of.

Interpretation is inevitable because of the nature of people. Have you ever heard anyone tell a joke which you already knew? Chances are that the joke teller reinterpreted, rephrased, or reemphasized the original joke. He may have added to, deleted from, or otherwise altered the joke. He may even have forgotten the punch line. The same things happen with rumor, gossip, or anything that is passed by word of mouth rather than by the written word. When we tell a story, we put in our own little prejudices, discriminations, tastes, values, and desires.

The task, then, of speaking written words aloud is to be so exact that the writer's message will not be distorted. You will almost have to say the words the way the author intended if you've read and thought carefully.

For example, in the paragraph you read earlier from Kurt Vonnegut, Jr., there are the key words used in the conversation—*industry, rules, managers, efficiency*—as well as punctuation that approximates as closely as possible the pauses, stops, and starts that Vonnegut used. By thinking about the meaning of each key word, and by using the punctuation as a guide, you can read the passage aloud as an exciting piece of oral interpretation.

To illuminate the meaning of a passage, any speaker must first have a clear understanding of every word used. You must examine the passage for the tone with which it was originally written or spoken. For example, looking again at the Vonnegut passage, you can see he has used no words which you do not know. However, their real meanings come from the ways he has used them—from his tone, from his attitude about the subject of the passage. In his first sentence he describes an industry "which no longer exists." Why do you think he put that phrase in the statement about the source of his training? Why does he use the word *industry*? Is he passing a judgment on the industry? Do you think of a writer of short stories as working in an industry? What is implied in the use of that word and that clause?

Only by understanding the selections of words a writer or speaker has made can you really understand the meaning of his sentences and therefore be able to say a sentence aloud with the interpretation necessary to carry the meaning. I would like you to continue reading aloud the conversation with Kurt Vonnegut, Jr., and to interpret the entire exchange by thinking about the words and phrasing he has chosen.

Let me slash up a passage so that I can give you some help with the phrasing. Take the following section:

> I learned that lesson so well/ and it is so automatic with me now when I write/ that when a character speaks,/ he either advances the story/ or reveals something significant about himself,/ or he does not speak./ This makes for efficiency;/ I don't know whether it makes for art.

Why do you suppose I didn't put a slash between *now* and *when* in the first sentence? Would you say the three phrases—*he either advances the story, or reveals something significant about himself, or he does not speak*—in the same way? I assume not, and you should not say them the same way. One is to be said quite differently from the other two. Do you know which one and why? What is the difference in interpretation when you say them all in the same way and when you say one phrase with an emphasis different from the emphasis given the others?

Let me take another paragraph, this time from the speech you read earlier by Adlai Stevenson. Examine the paragraph for its meaning:

> For the South/ this period was a desert without an oasis./ But,/ however hard it was to bear at the time,/ we in the more fortunate present/ can view it with a semblance of charity./ For the Republican leadership did not neglect the South and other Democrats/ simply because you were Democrats./

> In its frozen impartiality/ it also neglected Republican farmers,/ small businessmen,/ and working people./ Men earned the neglect of the Republican leaders/ not by their political affiliation,/ but by being small and poor./ And this is why so many people have shifted to the Democratic Party.

The first guide for you to use in sifting out the meaning is to check on all the words. Are there any that you don't know? Notice how Stevenson has used particular words and special phrasing: *however hard, semblance of charity, frozen impartiality, men earned the neglect.* He uses *neglect* three times in one paragraph. Why? The phrasing provides emphasis, as does pausing you use when you read the passage aloud. The most difficult clues, however, are in the tone. And tone is frequently where the secret to the meaning lies. What is Stevenson's tone here? Is he being sarcastic? Or does he think the Republicans have been impartial and fair? Is he interested in being charitable? Or is he being critical and condemning?

Tone is the author's or speaker's attitude toward his material. It is the single most difficult aspect of reading and speaking in oral interpretation. You have already experienced the problem of tone by the time you say to someone, or someone says to you, "But I was only kidding." What clues do you have when someone says this? Has the person been sarcastic? Was the speaker putting you on? Communication is totally dependent upon the tone in which something is *said* and *received.*

Here is one more paragraph for you to read aloud. It comes from a conversation I had with Dustin Hoffman which you'll read in the next chapter of this book. This time, you can supply the pauses:

> I love the writer to read. I remember I was an assistant director on a production of *View from the Bridge* years ago, and Arthur Miller read the play, doing all the parts. It seemed to be a shorthand for the actor—not that the actor would have performed the part as Arthur Miller read it, but it was a shorthand because you knew what he was getting at. I think we'd all be in for a big surprise if dead, great playwrights were around—if Shakespeare was around—to read. Maybe he'd read very differently from the way his plays are done. He was a very commercial guy in his day, you know.

Hoffman's attitude is made clear immediately by his use of the word *love*. He is very direct in his communication, and his tone is unmistakable until he begins talking about dead, great playwrights coming alive. Implied in his speculations that their works would be interpreted and produced differently from custom is the desire that their works be presented less pompously, less pretentiously, and less presumptuously than is the custom. Look at the words in the last line of Hoffman's statement. He uses colloquial language, colloquial expression—everything he can to minimize the "special" nature usually associated with Shakespeare.

Capturing the tone and meaning in prose is usually much easier than doing so in poetry. In fact, the poet Archibald MacLeish once wrote that a poem should not mean but be. Poetry is not very popular among adults, although children seem to love rhyme, and we all know that the best way to remember the calendar is by the verse "Thirty days hath September."

Many people are discouraged from reading poems because they feel that they can't understand them, or that they don't know how to react to them. Many people feel the same way about painting and classical music as well. Each form has its strengths and its weaknesses, and poetry is no exception. However, there is nothing alien or foreign about poetry, for it is one of the oldest forms of oral expression we know of. And poems are meant to be read aloud, to be "sung."

Obviously, there are funny poems which are certain to please everyone—usually because they are short, because they play with words in unusual ways, and because they make us laugh. My son David recently received a gift certificate to a local hamburger restaurant, and, when forced by his mother to send a thank-you note, decided to do so by writing the poem which follows:

> The trip to McDonald's,
> I surmise,
> Was an invitation
> That was very wise.
> Although the hamburgers
> Were not filet mignon,

>And the milkshakes
>Were not Saint-Emilion,
>The french fries were very good.

As is clear from this rhyme, poems are appropriate for all occasions. Just think of the greeting card business. I would like you to try a few rhymes (or unrhymes, if you wish) on any of the following subjects:

>Getting up in the morning
>Not being able to fall asleep
>Listening to music
>My idea of marriage
>When my teacher leaves work
>Returning from a vacation
>Not being invited to a party

And I would like you to try one more activity. Write a series of lines, rhymed or unrhymed, each line starting with one of the following:

>I wish
>I saw
>I am afraid that
>I wonder when (*or* if)

Now, take any one of your poems and read it aloud in front of a mirror. The best way for you to learn to read another writer's poems is to read aloud some that you have written yourself. Writing poetry does not require that you be a magician or a genius. It is a chance to have fun.

To get the sound and sense out of the poetry you read, you may wish to keep these fundamentals in mind:

1. Trust the material. The poet has selected specific words to do the job he thinks has to be done. Your emphasis on certain words and phrases is a matter of your interpretation, understanding, and taste, but your emphasis does not have to do the whole job. Words that strike your fancy as being more important than others should be emphasized by you, but not punched up—that is, don't overemphasize them, although

there may be a great temptation to do so. Through you, the poem should speak for itself.

2. Poetry is most closely allied to music. Rhythm in poetry is in the words and their organization. You don't have to impose rhythm on a poem; instead you should try to discover its natural rhythm and go along with it much as you would with any song.

3. Poetry is an economical use of language. The poet chooses particular words and phrases that say in the briefest manner what he wishes to express. Because the rest of us tend to use so many words, poetry sometimes confuses us, embarrasses us, even angers us. Trust the words of a poem as the genuine expression of the poet, and reveal the *poet*, not *you*. Examine the economical way in which the poet expressed himself.

4. Poets tend to compare the familiar with the unfamiliar. Metaphor is the comparison of the unfamiliar with the familiar to make meaning more clear. That doesn't mean that the poet lives in a fantasy world, but rather that he may see things in ways that we are not accustomed to. William Butler Yeats writes in a poem you'll read on the following page, "a fire was in my head." You and I know that he did not have a fire in his head, but instead that he had an intensity of feeling that could be compared to fire. Such is the language of poetry.

5. Poets tend to make pictures rather than to state facts. For instance, I could say to you that "all men are doomed to be unsatisfied despite the fact that most of us have much satisfaction in our lives." I could also say to you, "All rivers run into the sea, and the sea is never full." The second statement is a line of poetry from the Bible, and it creates an image or picture in your mind which my line cannot possibly create. Rather than be annoyed at the poet's desire to create images, try to capture them so that you can interpret the pictures as well as the words of a poem.

Apply these principles for finding sense and sound to the following poem. Trust the poet and listen to his sense. Don't worry if the poem bewilders you at first:

The Song of Wandering Aengus

I went out to the hazel wood,
Because a fire was in my head,
And cut and peeled a hazel wand,
And hooked a berry to a thread;
And when white moths were on the wing,
And moth-like stars were flickering out,
I dropped the berry in a stream
And caught a little silver trout.

When I had laid it on the floor
I went to blow the fire a-flame,
But something rustled on the floor,
And someone called me by my name:
It had become a glimmering girl
With apple blossom in her hair
Who called me by my name and ran
And faded through the brightening air.

Though I am old with wandering
Through hollow lands and hilly lands,
I will find out where she has gone,
And kiss her lips and take her hands;
And walk among long dappled grass,
And pluck till time and times are done,
The silver apples of the moon,
The golden apples of the sun.

William Butler Yeats

Notice, first of all, how Yeats has used color in his poem *(fire, white, silver, golden)*. Form your impression of the poem. Read it aloud. Does it sound singsongy to you? The language is indeed very simple, and the poem is written with a very regular beat. The beat makes you emphasize certain words—for example, the first line has an accent on *went, to, ha-,* and *wood.* The temptation might be for you to singsong that line made up of alternate beats. I suggest you try to avoid that by minimizing the regularity of the beat and maximizing your *sense* of the line.

A poet is conversing with his readers. As a sayer of a poem, speak it as if you were telling someone a story. Examine the economy, the words, and the images. Take a poem at face value rather than trying to find out what is profound in it. If the experience of the poet is profound, it will be in the telling of it for any listener to get. The speaker doesn't have to make sure that the audience gets it.

What is the experience of the narrator in Yeats's poem? Obviously, there is fantasy in the poem, but what can you find in the experience of this poem that you can compare to experiences in your life? Does your knowledge of that experience help you say the words with more sense? Again, don't worry about getting total meaning. Poets are re-creating experiences. Experiences relate to your emotions more than to your intellectual capacities. To help you get the sense of this poem, apply the principles of pausing, phrasing, and emphasis, just as you did with the prose passages earlier in this chapter. Try to get the feel of the words.

Look now at the next poem, and think, as you read it, how you might apply the same principles you've just read about:

Love's Secret

Never seek to tell thy love;
Love that never told can be;
For the gentle wind does move
Silently, invisibly.

I told my love, I told my love,
I told her all my heart;
Trembling, cold, in ghastly fears,
Ah! she doth depart.

Soon as she was gone from me,
A traveler came by,
Silently, invisibly:
He took her with a sigh.

William Blake

Does this poem tell you a story? What is the major experience in that story? If you want to know just how dramatic this poem can be, look for a copy of Tennessee Williams's play *Summer and Smoke.* You'll find that his play is actually a dramatization of Blake's poem.

Can you speak the words without being singsongy? Can you say the words as an expression of the poem's title, "Love's Secret"? Does the repetition of certain words such as *silently, invisibly* influence how you will say those words? Does an image come to your mind when you read the line "Trembling, cold, in ghastly fears"? How would you describe that image? Is the experience of the poem something that is familiar to you? Has the poet said it in such an unfamiliar way that your familiar experience is illuminated? In other words, does the poet help you to see something in your own life through the story he tells in this poem?

The next poem is about a young woman's dreams, but it is just as applicable to a young man's dreams. As you read the poem, ask which particular words and phrases give you clues to the sense of the poem. Imagine the poem being sung by one girl or one boy, perhaps accompanied by a guitar.

Departure

It's little I care what path I take,
    And where it leads it's little I care;
But out of this house, lest my heart break,
    I must go, and off somewhere.

It's little I know what's in my heart,
    What's in my mind it's little I know,
But there's that in me must up and start,
    And it's little I care where my feet go.

I wish I could walk for a day and a night,
    And find me at dawn in a desolate place
With never the rut of a road in sight,
    Nor the roof of a house, nor the eyes of a face.

I wish I could walk till my blood should spout,
    And drop me, never to stir again,
On a shore that is wide, for the tide is out,
    And the weedy rocks are bare to the rain.

But dump or dock, where the path I take
    Brings up, it's little enough I care;
And it's little I'd mind the fuss they'll make,
    Huddled dead in a ditch somewhere.

"Is something the matter, dear," she said,
    "That you sit at your work so silently?"
"No, mother, no, 'twas a knot in my thread.
    There goes the kettle, I'll make the tea."

Edna St. Vincent Millay

Does the rhythm of this poem hinder your being able to read it aloud with the proper sense? What about the final stanza? Can you read italics aloud? How will you interpret orally the last stanza to express the author's intentions? Once again, apply the principles of pausing, phrasing, and emphasis. Does the poem make sense to you?

Write your own poem called "Arrival," and see if you can articulate for yourself some feelings comparable to the ones Edna St. Vincent Millay has just registered for you.

The following poem is a narrative poem, a dramatic narrative in verse form. There are two voices to be heard, the husband's and the wife's. The poem may be read in class by two students, much in the same way as you would read a play.

Home Burial

He saw her from the bottom of the stairs
Before she saw him. She was starting down,
Looking back over her shoulder at some fear.
She took a doubtful step and then undid it

To raise herself and look again. He spoke
Advancing toward her: "What is it you see
From up there always—for I want to know."
She turned and sank upon her skirts at that,
And her face changed from terrified to dull.
He said to gain time: "What is it you see,"
Mounting until she cowered under him.
"I will find out now—you must tell me, dear."
She, in her place, refused him any help
With the least stiffening of her neck and silence.
She let him look, sure that he wouldn't see,
Blind creature; and awhile he didn't see.
But at last he murmured, "Oh," and again, "Oh."

"What is it—what?" she said.

                    "Just that I see."

"You don't," she challenged. "Tell me what it is."

"The wonder is I didn't see at once.
I never noticed it from here before.
I must be wonted to it—that's the reason.
The little graveyard where my people are!
So small the window frames the whole of it.
Not so much larger than a bedroom, is it?
There are three stones of slate and one of marble,
Broad-shouldered little slabs there in the sunlight
On the sidehill. We haven't to mind *those*.
But I understand: it is not the stones,
But the child's mound—"

            "Don't, don't, don't, don't," she cried.

She withdrew shrinking from beneath his arm
That rested on the bannister, and slid downstairs;
And turned on him with such a daunting look,
He said twice over before he knew himself:
"Can't a man speak of his own child he's lost?"

"Not you! Oh, where's my hat? Oh, I don't need it!
I must get out of here. I must get air.
I don't know rightly whether any man can."

"Amy! Don't go to someone else this time.
Listen to me. I won't come down the stairs."
He sat and fixed his chin between his fists.
"There's something I should like to ask you, dear."

"You don't know how to ask it."

                "Help me, then."

Her fingers moved the latch for all reply.

"My words are nearly always an offense.
I don't know how to speak of anything
So as to please you. But I might be taught
I should suppose. I can't say I see how.
A man must partly give up being a man
With women-folk. We could have some arrangement
By which I'd bind myself to keep hands off
Anything special you're a-mind to name.
Though I don't like such things 'twixt those that love.
Two that don't love can't live together without them.
But two that do can't live together with them."
She moved the latch a little. "Don't—don't go.
Don't carry it to someone else this time.
Tell me about it if it's something human.
Let me into your grief. I'm not so much
Unlike other folks as your standing there
Apart would make me out. Give me my chance.
I do think, though, you overdo it a little.
What was it brought you up to think it the thing
To take your mother-loss of a first child
So inconsolably—in the face of love.
You'd think his memory might be satisfied—"

"There you go sneering now!"

                              "I'm not, I'm not!
You make me angry. I'll come down to you.
God, what a woman! And it's come to this,
A man can't speak of his own child that's dead."

"You can't because you don't know how to speak.
If you had any feelings, you that dug
With your own hand — how could you? — his little grave;
I saw you from that very window there,
Making the gravel leap and leap in air,
Leap up, like that, like that, and land so lightly
And roll back down the mound beside the hold.
I thought, Who is that man? I didn't know you.
And I crept down the stairs and up the stairs
To look again, and still your spade kept lifting.
Then you came in. I heard your rumbling voice
Out in the kitchen, and I don't know why,
But I went near to see with my own eyes.
You could sit there with the stains on your shoes
Of the fresh earth from your own baby's grave
And talk about your everyday concerns.
You had stood the spade up against the wall
Outside there in the entry, for I saw it."

"I shall laugh the worst laugh I ever laughed.
I'm cursed. God, if I don't believe I'm cursed."

"I can repeat the very words you were saying.
'Three foggy mornings and one rainy day
Will rot the best birch fence a man can build.'
Think of it, talk like that at such a time!
What had how long it takes a birch to rot
To do with what was in the darkened parlor.
You *couldn't* care! The nearest friends can go
With anyone to death, comes so far short
They might as well not try to go at all.
No, from the time when one is sick to death,
One is alone, and he dies more alone.

Friends make pretense of following to the grave,
But before one is in it, their minds are turned
And making the best of their way back to life
And living people, and things they understand.
But the world's evil. I won't have grief so
If I can change it. Oh, I won't. I won't!"

"There, you have said it all and you feel better.
You won't go now. You're crying. Close the door.
The heart's gone out of it: why keep it up.
Amy! There's someone coming down the road!"

"*You*—oh, you think the talk is all. I must go—
Somewhere out of this house. How can I make you—"

"If—you—do!" She was opening the door wider.
"Where do you mean to go? First tell me that.
I'll follow and bring you back by force. I *will!*—"

Robert Frost

Frost uses everyday language in his poem about a farm couple in an earlier time, perhaps the beginning of this century. The farm couple, presumably New Englanders, would traditionally have been people of few words and many thoughts. Does that tradition apply in this poem? Do you get the sense of both people? Say this poem in your own words so you understand what is clear to you and what is not clear. What things has Frost purposely left out or only implied? What do you begin to surmise by the end of the poem? How does that revelation influence the way you would read both the man's voice and the woman's voice?

I would like you to go to the library and find some poems—any poems—that make sense to you. You may find poems that are song lyrics printed on the album covers of records that you like. Choose any poems that you are willing to say aloud to your class because you would like to share with the class your experience at discovering some new voices. Discovery is exciting, and you should be having that experience frequently. Don't deny yourself the pleasure.

Making Contact with Dustin Hoffman

Dustin Hoffman spent many years studying his craft as an actor before gaining recognition. Although he began acting at the age of nineteen, it was ten years before he won attention for his performance in the off-Broadway play *The Journey of the Fifth Horse*. In his first film performance, he played Benjamin Braddock in *The Graduate*. That performance was followed by his role as Ratso Rizzo in *Midnight Cowboy*. He then made the film *John and Mary*, followed by *Little Big Man*, in which he played Jack Crabb from age sixteen to 121. Hoffman later returned to Broadway for the musical *Jimmy Shine*. He then made the film *Straw Dogs*. With Paul McCluskey of Harcourt Brace Jovanovich, I talked to Dustin Hoffman in New York City in October, 1972, shortly before he went to Spain to film *Papillon*.

STEIN

Who decides how you say your dialogue? You? The director? Both of you?

HOFFMAN

I think every actor worth his salt has a silent war with the director, no matter who the director is. You can say the line the way the director wants it to be said and the way the writer has written it, and that may move a play along. But the life of the moment will be deadened if it's just coming by rote. Acting, for me, is mainly concerned with being alive, with communicating a spontaneity to an audience. So the line will differ from night to night, and if *anyone* will decide how the line should be said, it will be the other actor who says the line preceding the line you say, or it will come from an inner impulse independent of the other actor. Most actors complain about being in a play for a year. I think that's simply because the lines become set. It's the natural thing to do in life, I think — to become set. I do it in my everyday life, and we all fight against it.

STEIN

It's very tempting to become a technician, because technical life is very comfortable and it's very safe.

HOFFMAN

Lately I've been going to see documentary film footage shot in prisons because of a project I'm interested in. As you watch the footage, you see the choices that one could make as an actor that actors never make, and you see the choices that could be directorial that directors never make because they are the antithesis of what we are accustomed to knowing. In life, even if we're not actors, having grown up in a movie culture, our reflexes seem conditioned by movies. So that it's not impossible that one will be at a funeral for one's father and very quickly think, *I better cry*, because Arthur Kennedy cried when his father Lee Cobb died in that movie, or Deborah Kerr cried, or we know that crying is associated with funerals. And yet Pennebaker, the documentary film maker, will tell you that he has shot funerals where people start giggling and laughing.

STEIN

I wonder if you could tell me if there are any clues the writer gives you about how you say your lines in the performance of a play?

HOFFMAN

Well, I can speak only for myself. I don't want to say this is the way it *should* be: I always jump to the chance of having the writer read his play. I love the writer to read. I remember I was an assistant director on a production of *View from the Bridge* years ago, and Arthur Miller read the play, doing all the parts. It seemed to be a shorthand for the actor—not that the actor would have performed the part as Arthur Miller read it, but it was a shorthand because you knew what he was getting at. I think we'd all be in for a big surprise if dead, great playwrights were around—if Shakespeare was around—to read. Maybe he'd read very differently from the way his plays are done. He was a very commercial guy in his day, you know.

STEIN

You once told a *Life* interviewer that the hardest part of playing a 121-year-old man in *Little Big Man* was getting the voice right. I wonder why you considered the voice to be so important?

HOFFMAN

The voice was important because he was narrating throughout the film. It wasn't just a scene in the beginning and then we lose him; his voice stayed through the whole film, and we wanted to have a particular kind of voice that would immediately create the image. While the audience was watching the film, when the audience heard the narrating voice, it would create the image of this cantankerous old man. I don't think that was achieved, by the way. I don't think I did that. When I saw the film for myself, it disturbed me that the image was not sharp enough. I wanted it to really sound like someone 121 years old. Well, in a way when I think back on it, that wasn't important really. What was important was that it sound *mythically* like one would sound at 121. It should have been like a Daumier caricature. I never did find a way to do it. I went to geriatric homes and taped people who were in their nineties. That didn't help me too much. I talked to surgeons who dealt with people who had impaired larynxes, and doctors told me what happens to the voice when it gets old and why it has that rasp. Then, one day in the middle of shooting (we were not going to shoot the old man until the last part of the shooting), I got sick and was working with a virus and a slight case of laryngitis. I quickly put myself on tape, and thought, *That's it. Now all I have to do is get sick when we shoot because that's exactly what I want.* But I couldn't get sick. What I did was scream and yell for three or four solid hours each morning before shooting started, because I didn't want to *act* it, I wanted it to be there naturally. The voice box is very resilient, I guess, because I was hoarse for a few hours and then slowly my voice would come back. Luckily, I just had to do the speech for three days. I don't recommend that approach. It's not the craft as we know it, but I didn't find any other way to do it.

STEIN

There are not a lot of roles written for 121-year-old people.

HOFFMAN

No. I don't know how I would do it on Broadway every night. In fact, I wrote to Hal Holbrook, who I had seen do Mark Twain, and to me that performance was magic. But he wouldn't give up any secrets. He sent back a letter and said, *You're a fine actor and I'm sure you'll find your own way.*

STEIN

When you were in the play *The Journey of the Fifth Horse*, it's reported that you were having trouble getting into the character you were playing. During previews you started one performance with a strange, tight-lipped voice and realized that that voice was precisely right to express the character's desperation. In other words, the voice gave you the *key* to the character.

HOFFMAN

Yes. I don't think the voice is the paramount thing. It's one, and the body is another. Most important, I think, is understanding the core of a character, and that is an emotional experience that happens or doesn't happen in the course of rehearsal. When it happens, everything comes—voice, body, rhythm. In the play, I was working in my usual way, which is distrustful of anybody pushing me faster than I care to go. It's very selfish, because you hold up other actors. I think maybe you should have more responsibility to other actors, but at the same time try not to disturb your own process of work. And the process of *not* knowing is important—not demanding anything of yourself, but just going through it, feeling your way until something starts to hit. I think it *has* to happen. Things *have* to start to hit. The actor, or director, can't decide that in the first week of rehearsal. The success is in the surprises we find out. By the time we were in previews, I could connect very strongly with the character for some reason. I was on to him. He was a little man, like myself, and I was in connection with a lot of psychological things about him. But I always felt that something was missing. Suddenly there was an audience and I had my costume on and my make-up—everything. And this was the first play that was going to be reviewed that I had done after being in New York for almost ten years. Backstage, a girl asked me, *Are you nervous?* I said, *The voice, I don't know how to talk. There's something that I feel he should have, like a British accent. But he can't. Yet, something's missing.* I went onstage in a kind of fright, and suddenly this voice came out of me which I had not done in rehearsal, but must have been thinking about without realizing. It was a very high-pitched, nasal voice. Very clipped. It had the essence of being very upper-class British without being British. *Very precise.* And it seemed too much. It seemed startling to me. And it startled the other actors. After the first long scene, when I went offstage, they said, *What are you doing? Are you out of your mind?* And I said to myself, *I can't drop it now. I have to continue doing it for the rest of the play!* And I did. And that voice became the expressive part of the character. Maybe one doesn't describe himself so much by his voice as he *betrays* himself by it. It was important for this character to betray himself by his voice. In his mind he was a little man who wanted power very much, but he had a low estimation of himself. So he compensated by sounding, in his own mind, very authoritative. What came across was the fear and absurdity of this little pipsqueak going around in this almost Hitlerian way. It was a great experience. Everything started to happen, to blossom, because I felt I *sounded* right.

STEIN

Did things start happening with other members of the cast, as well as with yourself?

HOFFMAN

With some good members of the cast, I guess. The bad actors don't change, no matter what you do. I think every actor who has to take over a role has experienced this. The actors have been playing for six months with Joe Blow, and suddenly you are playing the role somewhat differently simply because you're a different person. Bad actors will respond to you the same way they responded to Joe Blow. But good actors will play off you. Writers will sometimes say, *The character began to write himself.* And I think that happens sometimes in acting. You begin to surprise yourself, and you become less self-conscious of what you're doing.

McCLUSKEY

How did you learn to talk like Ratso in *Midnight Cowboy*? Was it easier once you were made up to look like him, or didn't that matter?

HOFFMAN

I always think the best thing in acting is not to know how the character is going to turn out for you. At the very beginning, if you know *I'm going to end up with this kind of a walk, that kind of a voice,* you're in trouble. With Ratso, I knew one thing: I wasn't interested in doing a real Ratso. I wanted, in a sense, to do *all* the Ratsos, so I wanted to lift it a little bit. Or, if you will, stylize it. It's not a cartoon or a caricature, but somehow an impression of *all* the Ratsos that are in *all* of us. The decisions about how he would walk and talk sparked from that. I would walk down the street and watch people limp day after day after day, and finally the limp that I wound up with was a combination of limps that I had put together. Now, the voice: the writer of the book, James Leo Herlihy, wrote that Ratso had grown up in the Bronx of Italian parentage in a Jewish neighborhood, and I kind of liked that. So the character had a lower-class New York accent that was half Italian lower class, half Jewish lower class, which is kind of peculiar to New York—that combination of dialects. I liked fooling around with that. I wanted the character to have a dignity about him. The character was depressing me, and I felt my own desire was to bring myself out of the depression by creating a sense of dignity to lift me. Now, the other things you suggest were important to develop Ratso physically. I started to comb my hair back, and I had a plate of teeth made that I could just clip on

because I wanted the teeth to be dirty. But when I put the teeth in and began rehearsing, I found that it affected my speech, and instead of fighting that reality, I just went with it and found myself not only talking differently, but certain feelings of character, if you will, began emerging. In a way that was part of the creation of the voice. The voice became a very important part of the character because it was his means of expressing dignity. He knew what he looked like. He knew that he limped. He was super aware of that. The voice was a way of cutting through, of gaining not only dignity, but attention. At times the voice was sort of proud and piercing. I always had an image of Ratso as being a survivor in a concentration camp, one of those guys who, when the war was over, would be standing up against the wire fence.

STEIN

Do you think it's important, or right, in an actor's development for him to be able to articulate some of these things about the characters he plays?

HOFFMAN

I think a very important thing is never to be easily satisfied, never to con yourself. I have to know that I'm never going to completely accomplish what I set out to do, because what I set out to do in my mind is impossible — to try to be another human being. That doesn't mean that I can't go for it, and, with total commitment, perhaps get very close, but I have to start out with the premise that I'm never going to reach it. I can't portray another human being 100 percent. So I can only portray telling *aspects* of the character. It may give an audience the impression that I really did it. But I really didn't.

McCLUSKEY

You merely approximate Ratso. You're not really Ratso?

HOFFMAN

Right. Ratso doesn't exist, really, so you create him. You give an impression of him. It may be more exciting to do it that way. Real scrutiny is open scrutiny. You stand on a street corner watching a man nod from a heroin fix. He seems to be going down so far, then he stops, then he comes back up again, then he goes down a little bit more, he never touches the ground, and then comes back up. You're watching all of these things. You could watch that for an hour, and then if you had to play the part, you could get onstage and approximate that, and it would be valid. But there's something in your scrutiny which demands *more* than that—that you not only be able to reproduce literally what you've seen through scrutiny, but somehow that it begins to affect you, and you then translate it. So that your junkie is different from anyone else's junkie. You begin to get into that man who is nodding.

STEIN

That's a leap, a gigantic leap.

HOFFMAN

In a way it is. But it's not something that you should have to consciously do. The leap takes care of itself. You make that leap in fantasy and become the bank robber, the prostitute, the figure of authority. It's a marvelous feeling to suddenly get the shakes from having read something or having observed something. You get the shakes because you start to identify closely with it. Now, whatever it is that gives you the shakes is what makes you want to play the part. In the documentaries I've watched lately, I see people who are condemned prisoners facing the gas chamber or the electric chair. Somewhere in me there is a desire to try to experience that as an actor. There is such a close identification with the material that I literally come out shaking a little bit. Now, I know that is the germ of something. And I want to take off and connect with the experience.

STEIN

Can you express changing age by changing speech?

HOFFMAN

I'm not good at it. I saw John Gielgud one time reciting T. S. Eliot's poetry. His voice struck me as being kind of slick and technical. Then, suddenly, I found that I was crying, and I was aware for the first time that I was reacting to the very thing I had always disliked—a tremendous technical facility which I think can sometimes be sterile. But Gielgud was quite effective. Somehow there was that great technical equipment, but there was an emotional commitment with it. He seemed to me to be changing his voice in an almost mechanical way from verse to verse, and it worked because he happened to be extraordinary. He was painting, using all that technical equipment and yet was emotionally committed at the same time.

STEIN

In making a movie done over many months and shot out of sequence, how do you maintain the continuity of the character you're playing?

HOFFMAN

Ideally, every actor and, I guess, every director would like to shoot in continuity, starting the first day with the first scene of the movie and ending the last day with the last scene. The reason this isn't done is simply because of money. Things are shot out of continuity because it's cheaper to, say, shoot all interiors at one time, or all exteriors at one time. Even though films are shot out of continuity, there is one thing which you don't have on the stage—*rushes,* which are tremendously exciting to me. You can see what you did the day before in rushes. You can watch and gauge your performance that way. However, the problem remains: you can't rehearse day after day, week after week, and then open as you do in a play. When you do that, you grow with the play, and it becomes very exciting. Some film directors are powerful enough and smart enough to change some of the limitations of film making. Mike Nichols is an example. In filming *The Graduate,* he did two things which were, at that time, unheard of for directors to do: he rehearsed the entire film on a sound stage for a month with all the principal actors—it could have opened as a play on the day we started shooting the film—and he shot at least 60 percent of the film in continuity. It cost a lot more money to do that, but the sense of continuity was very important.

McCLUSKEY

Do you look back on *The Graduate* and the technique that Nichols used there as something you would like to see repeated in other films you do, or have you become accustomed to a different kind of shooting schedule?

HOFFMAN

No, I still like that. Schlesinger did the same thing with *Midnight Cowboy.* We rehearsed for nearly three weeks. I always think it's valuable to rehearse. You discover major elements about the character you're playing. If you made those discoveries after a month's shooting, you couldn't change the character because it would distort what was already on film.

STEIN

There's a phenomenal paradox of acting: you can't *be* Othello, because you would kill Desdemona if you were Othello, but you have to be Othello if you're going to convince me out there in the audience that he's a real person.

HOFFMAN

You have to find something that you can believe in, as an actor, that will equal the thing that you're doing. You know you can't really strangle Desdemona, but you can find something that you can really believe at that moment that has the passion of the moment. One teacher told me when I first started out, *You don't have to be a killer to kill.* You have to find in yourself those moments in your own life when you could really kill—moments of pure rage that you can re-create onstage. I've found there is no moment of greater rage for me than being awakened in the middle of the night by a mosquito buzzing around. Since childhood I've always turned on the light and, if necessary, spent three hours looking for that mosquito, and when I find it there is a tremendous delight in hitting it. If you can pretend that there is a mosquito on Desdemona's neck, you can experience all the rage Othello felt.

STEIN

Would you ever consider a leading part that called for no dialogue at all?

HOFFMAN

I've always liked parts that have little dialogue, because I just like to communicate in ways that aren't verbal. One good thing about films is that they don't rely as much on dialogue as plays do. I've always seemed to bend toward physical action. I really am envious of that whole period of silent films. If I would've been around then, it would have been maybe more stimulating for me.

STEIN

Do you enjoy the inventiveness that is necessary there? Obviously, you must be terribly inventive to communicate without using words.

HOFFMAN

Well, physical stuff has just always appealed to me. I've had a lot of training—in my grammar school, in junior high school, and high school—where you couldn't talk in class and you had to find ways of communicating, of making the kids laugh, without being heard. I had a rich training period. I still carry it through now, I guess, when I can communicate in a nonverbal way.

STEIN

How different is acting only to a camera from interacting with other actors on a stage?

HOFFMAN

The camera makes me self-conscious, especially in close-ups when it's right up your nostrils. In close-ups, the other actor is off camera. He sticks his head right up to the side of the camera, and you talk right past the lens to him. I've always wanted the actor to be there. Many actors, especially in the old days, would just talk to the script clerk, or just talk to a knob, and have the lines thrown off to them.

STEIN

You want a sense of reality, then?

HOFFMAN

I would like it, and I like it when I'm off camera. I think a lot of film actors will tell you that they give their best performances when they're off camera, because they're relaxed.

McCLUSKEY

If you were doing a scene which was a close-up of only your face, and your hands and feet were tied, could you still act?

HOFFMAN

No, I don't think so. It's important to be able to move. Many times you do get frozen because you can't move or the lighting will be off. Nowadays, a good director will foresake a particular kind of lighting to get more natural behavior on the screen. The director will say, *Let him move. I want the performance to have a life to it. Let's give up the other things.* I think it's more important to have a good performance than a pretty picture.

STEIN

Have you discovered that stage and film make different demands on your voice?

HOFFMAN

There is a difference. On the stage, words are so much more important to give a feeling of intimacy that will extend even to the people in the balcony. Film can communicate that intimacy without words. The audience is simply not as intimate with the stage, even though it's live. A play seen from the second balcony is a different play altogether from a play seen from the second or third row. Words play a very important part on the stage because they communicate a tremendous amount of the emotional impact of the play. In films—Buster Keaton once said this in an interview—if you can find a way of saying, *I love you,* without having to really say it, you're better off. It's much more exciting. Film is a medium that is not so dependent on words. It's an extraordinary medium with this seventy-foot screen filled with one face. You can communicate even to the back row of the theater. When I was doing *The Graduate,* after I had studied acting for ten years and acted two years on the stage, Mike Nichols would say to me over and over, *Don't do anything. Do nothing.* We'd do a take and he'd say, *Now, let's do it again. Do nothing.* And I was very offended by that. I said, *What? I put in all these years of study and now you're telling me to do nothing?* Well, what he meant was that, after all the improvisation, rehearsal, work on the scenes, if you then did nothing you were still going to be doing a lot because the screen is so big and the camera is so close. One of the exciting things about film is that you can make subtle choices that will not be seen on the stage. Yet, again, there are certain things that will work onstage but will not work in a film because they become too large, grotesque.

STEIN

Have you had much experience in improvisation?

HOFFMAN

The major part of an actor's training comes from what he does in life, not in class. We can improvise in life, whether we're actors or not. We play roles in different situations and improvise our way through them. We don't know the lines in life and yet we improvise. Once I started acting, I realized that the first thing that has to be there is the need in life to play-act. I always have been suspect of people who say, *Oh, if I couldn't be an actor, I would kill myself.* I've never quite believed that, because we all find ways of expressing ourselves, of fulfilling that need to be seen or heard. Before I ever started improvising in class, I was improvising in life. I'd get all kinds of different jobs and would improvise on my jobs. If I was a waiter, I would have a French accent. Sometimes I'd be unmasked: if I was doing the French accent well, a customer would start speaking French to me and I would then have to say, *I'm sorry, but I'm trying to learn the English language and I prefer not to speak my native tongue.* Improvisation is very much dependent upon the teacher or director, and many teachers and directors don't know enough about improvisations. It is very important that they be set up for specific reasons. They should be set up to help the actor explore some specific demand made upon him by the material he is dealing with. I think some improvisations can hurt, if not set up properly because they can lead to a kind of glib verbal response. It is my feeling that the audience *really* believes only when the actor *really* believes. However, both may be believing in different things. But I just want to say that acting to me is a very personal thing and though I've studied for many years with different teachers and different approaches, I find at this stage of the game that ultimately I have to discover for myself my *own* way of working, my *own* way of kicking myself off. A few years ago, I read an interview with Laurence Olivier. He was asked how he found a certain character in Shakespeare and he replied, *I tried many things and one day I went through the play imagining I was holding a green umbrella and suddenly the character was real to me.* Now, if I had to do a Shakespearean role and had gone out to Macy's and bought a green umbrella, I would have wound up with a green umbrella.

We are what we pretend to be,

In *When She Was Good,* Philip Roth wrote: "Because she could not understand the most basic fact of human life, the fact that I am me and you are you." As you read this chapter on acting, you may want to keep that sentence in mind.

Acting is pretending. Do you know much about pretending? You probably think pretending is phony, and it is. Acting in a way is being phony. Do you remember Dustin Hoffman saying the following about acting?

PUT ON ANOTHER FACE

I have to know that I'm never going to completely accomplish what I set out to do, because what I set out to do in my mind is impossible—to try to be another human being. That doesn't mean that I can't go for it, and, with total commitment, perhaps get very close, but I have to start out with the premise that I'm never going to reach it. I can't portray another human being 100 percent.

You can't portray another human being 100 percent. Yet, that is what acting is all about—pretending to be another human being.

so we must be careful about

Acting is also imitating. If you were asked to imitate members of your family, how would you go about it? Would you imitate their ways of walking? The words they use? The way they talk? The way they use their hands or eyes? Choose one member of your family, and try it. Chances are that you pick up a mannerism or eccentricity or idiosyncrasy—something that is peculiar to that member of your family alone.

what we pretend to be.

By doing that, you impersonate character. TV personalities do that very often. They imitate Ed Sullivan's nervous body movements, Jack Benny's funny walk, Marilyn Monroe's baby voice, President Nixon's favorite expression, "Let me make one thing perfectly clear."

I'd like you to impersonate one of your teachers or your principal or a student in your school whom most other students will recognize. You may be reluctant to do this activity because you may be afraid of hurting people's feelings. In fact, you may think that people who see themselves imitated or impersonated will be certain to object because of fear of ridicule or criticism. They should if you make fun of them. But there is also something to the statement "Imitation is the sincerest form of flattery." The fact is that all of us have our own special idiosyncrasies, and a good observer notices them. The best observer is that person who selects the idiosyncrasy which most clearly reflects the character or personality of the person being imitated. In a sense, an impersonator holds a mirror up to you when he imitates you, and you may be offended by what you see. Many of us are. But being able to take it is a sign of maturity and a willingness to grow in self-knowledge. Nobody is perfect, and everybody can use whatever information they can obtain that will help them to learn who they are.

If imitating someone close to you is too difficult because of sensitive feelings, try organizing a program at the end of the school year to say good-by to your school, a program packed with imitations of your schoolmates, teachers, administrators, janitors, and staff. Try it, and I'll bet you'll have fun. And so will they.

You might want to go outside your school to do impersonations, or impressions, as in the case of the next activity. Have you ever wanted to be someone else? Napoleon? Cleopatra? Joan of Arc? Moses? Joe Namath? Barbra Streisand? If you could be someone from history, who would you like to be? Pick out that person and imitate your hero or heroine. What is there in the person you've chosen that strikes you particularly? To answer this question, you must have observed something specific. It is that specific observation which is basic to acting.

Paul Newman told me once that when he was a student at the Yale School of Drama in New Haven, Connecticut, he used to go down to the bus station and watch all the people. He would observe the eccentricities of their movements, voices, and personalities, and he would listen to what they said. These observations became a storehouse of specifics for him when he later went into professional theater. A good actor is watching people all the time. He learns about people's character by watching particular behavior instead of general behavior. As you read the next few pages of this chapter, I'll be asking you to look ahead from time to time at the play "String" in the next chapter. If you have the time, you may want to read the play through first so that we will both be dealing with specifics. In the description of Joe in the play, the writer gives the following stage direction: "His walk is apologetic and uncertain." How would you act that direction? Would you be bent and shuffling? Stiff and stumbling? Crouched and hesitant? An actor with a storehouse of observations might have seen a particular walk on a particular man which he could imitate and make specific in his portrayal of Joe. Otherwise, the actor is likely to go right to the cliché of "apologetic and uncertain," a cliché which might suffice but which would give no individual quality to the Joe he was pretending to be.

I am asking you to watch the people around you. Watch how they walk, how they gesture, what words they use, what habits they employ as a means of getting their own way or getting out of work or getting attention. Make a record of your observations for yourself and practice imitations on the basis of what you have recorded.

Without any record, however, try the following activity in your own room or your own home. Consider yourself a janitor in a play. Sweep the floor. What eccentricities could you give that janitor to make him more interesting to an audience in a theater? Be patient. Give yourself time and see what you can come up with that would make him an appealing or colorful personality to an observer. Try some other activities like these. Be a parent telling a child to put on a coat before going outside. Be a son or daughter asking for money to go to the movies.

Thinking in specifics is one way to get close to your own character as well as the character you pretend to be when you act on a stage. You have to be in touch with your own feelings, as Dustin Hoffman told me. That requires specifics. Dustin Hoffman wanted to give Ratso specific qualities in *Midnight Cowboy,* just as you would want to give specific qualities to the character of Joe in "String." Specifics are the keys to characterization.

But specifics are not the complete answer by any means. It is a large task to discover character in the dialogue a writer has given a character. You and I can begin to scratch the surface of the problem, and I would begin my scratching by thinking again about what Dustin Hoffman said: you can portray only telling *aspects* of a character. A key to the aspects is in the principle that every dominant aspect has its opposite in the same person: Ratso is like a rat, but he also has dignity; the clerk in *The Journey of the Fifth Horse* is a pipsqueak who thirsts for power; Joe in "String" is apologetic and uncertain while at the same time obsessed with his honor. Look for the opposites in a character. Think about the following statement: inside every heavy, clumsy woman, a thin, delicate girl is screaming to get out; inside every aggressive, domineering man is a shy, withering boy. Ideal acting incorporates these opposites. Your portrayal may be limited to the dominant quality only, but it is always wise to try to understand the recessive quality also.

You might practice this by pretending to be just the opposite of what you consider yourself to be. For instance, if you consider yourself timid, shy, and somewhat withdrawn, pretend to be assertive or aggressive, pushy, and demanding. Create a situation for yourself that is connected with your family. Or take another situation: pretend you are in a long line at the movies waiting to buy tickets and a stranger comes up and says, "Do you mind if I get in front of you. I don't like to wait in line." How would you respond if you pretended to act in just the opposite way that you imagine you would act in a real situation?

Take still another situation. Pretend you are confronted at the front door of your school by a classmate who says, "Hurry, lend me your homework. I didn't have time to do it." Make arguments for yourself that are just the opposite of what you think you would probably do.

Perhaps I should give you an example of some dialogue for this last situation. Let us assume that ordinarily you would simply say, "Okay, here's what I did." But, because you are behaving in the opposite way for this activity, you would say, "No." The dialogue goes like this:

You: No.
Classmate: Why not?
You: It's my homework.
Classmate: But I need it.
You: Then why didn't you do it yourself?
Classmate: I told you. I didn't have time.
You: Tough.
Classmate: Stop being such a square.
You: You stop being such a pentagon.
Classmate: You're a creep, a rat, and a louse.
You: You're asking me to cheat.

Now it is possible in a real-life situation that you would hide your feeling that your classmate is imposing upon you by asking to count your homework as his own. You may not like to admit you would feel that because you probably want to believe you don't care that much about school or homework or being honest. But the chances are that somewhere deep inside you, you would resent your classmate's taking advantage of you. Maybe you don't want to make a big issue out of it, however. So you hide your true feelings, even though they are there. In such a case, you would have two contradictory feelings, even if your words only reveal one feeling. Or could you make your words indicate *both* feelings at once? Try the dialogue above again. Say the words for **You,** but say them as if you really want to give your homework to your classmate even though you also want to deny your classmate's request.

Although I have been talking about the recessive quality in a character, I must emphasize the necessity of locating and respecting the dominant feature, for it is that ruling passion which governs the identity of the character. In "String," the author gives a rather good series of clues in the description of Mrs. Rogers and Mrs. Beverly when she says, "Mrs. Rogers subtly suggests that she has a servant in Mrs. Beverly." The difference in their clothing (Mrs. Rogers wears a well-cut linen suit, appropriate for the sophisticated, higher-class lady she obviously considers herself to be, while Mrs. Beverly wears a splashy, colorful outfit like the more earthy woman that she is) gives you clues about the dominant qualities in the two ladies. Now go to Maydelle. The first clue we get to her dominant quality is that she respectfully refers to Joe as Mr. Joe. Then she demonstrates her warmth and compassion by consoling Joe in what must have been a tiff with the owner of the bar and grill. She even apologizes for the owner's behavior by saying, "He's not really drunk . . . just feelin' kind-a good." There we have clues to the warm, friendly, compassionate character of Maydelle. See if you can take the other three characters in "String" and isolate their dominant qualities. Where did you find your clues to describe Joe, L. V., and Katy? Once you have located the clues to each of those characters' dominant qualities, can you find clues for their recessive qualities?

A writer has three basic methods by which to develop a character: what other people in the play say about the character, what the character says, and what the character does. For example, take Maydelle again. The first thing we learn about Maydelle comes from a conversation between Mrs. Rogers and Mrs. Beverly who want her to be replaced as chairlady of the block association. These two fussy, complaining, and perhaps ambitious ladies are not particularly appealing, so we are left to believe that Maydelle may be more attractive than they are. And when she comes in and speaks to Joe and to the other characters, we are assured that Maydelle is indeed a likable, attractive, warm person. When Joe thanks Maydelle for giving him a free bus ticket and she denies having done so, she performs an act which makes her dominant character all the more firm. When she asks Joe to join the party under the tree, her act is again something that tells us about her character.

Of the three methods used by writers, the most revealing is what a character does. The secret to finding out what a character does in a play is to pick up the decisions the character makes. Those decisions are the character's actions, just as your decisions are the actions in your life. Actions in plays need not be big fights or murders or slamming of doors or shouting or noisy parties. The major actions by characters in plays are the decisions they make. Take any character in "String" or in a play you enjoy and isolate the decisions the character makes. For example, in "String," Joe decides to turn down the offer of whiskey from L. V., decides to sing, decides to pick up the string, decides not to tell the others he has picked up a piece of string, and so on. All these decisions tell you something about his character.

As you can see in this discussion, a character does not exist alone. A character exists in relationship to the other characters in a play. Before you try to act with someone, you might think it isn't very difficult to relate to another person on the stage. Once you attempt it, however, you will find out how difficult it is. You depend on that other character to bring out your own characterization, just as the other character, or characters, will depend upon you.

Let me offer you another activity to do. Take a classmate to the front of the room, place two chairs facing one another (more or less), and sit down with your classmate. Look at each other while you are both thinking about a happy moment in your lives. Reflect that happiness as naturally as you can. Now stop and do the same exercise, thinking about a sad, very sad, moment in your lives. Can you feel the difference in the two different situations with your classmate? Did you relate to your classmate in the same way in each situation? If not, what was the difference?

Sensing the feelings of another person is not something we are usually so conscious of doing. In acting, it is essential that you do this. Here are two activities that may illustrate my point for you:

First, set up two chairs back to back in front of your class to represent the locations of two telephones. In one chair you dial and start a conversation. Your opening line is, "I have a message that says you called me this afternoon, and I'm returning your call." Your classmate's answer is, "I didn't call you." Continue the conversation (because you have used the opening line as a means of getting attention and perhaps a date).

After completing this activity, push away the chairs and start walking toward each other. Just as you approach your classmate, say, "I understand you called me last night. I'm sorry I didn't return your call." Your classmate says, "I didn't call you. You must be mistaken." Continue the conversation, for once again you have tried to gain attention, and try to arrange for a date.

Was there a difference between the scene in which you were isolated back to back in a telephone conversation and the one in which you were facing each other? Relating onstage is a difficult task. It takes a great deal of listening and watching, as well as talking. Practice it.

One of the best ways to practice acting is through improvisation. Improvisation means creating a very brief plot or story and implementing it with dialogue that is not planned or rehearsed. You have already been doing improvisations in the activities I've suggested earlier in this chapter.

The value of improvisation is that it is spontaneous acting and frequently offers a professional actor a fresher sense of his character. A great danger exists in improvisation, however, for the actor is both the actor and the writer. Because of this danger, it is wise for the actor to have some basic facts established so that he doesn't aimlessly wander. For example, have your classmates join you in the following activity.

All of you are in an airport terminal and you are told that only ten of you are going to be allowed on the plane for which you are all waiting. Consider your teacher as the pilot, and convince the pilot of your need to be on board the plane.

Consider another situation. A woman is alone in her apartment. There is a loud knocking at her door and a frantic voice says, "Please let me in." She opens the door and finds a friend she has not seen for several years. The friend tells her that he is being chased by the police and asks her to hide him. Make up the scene, which should end when the police knock on the door.

For both of these improvisations, the secret is in your establishing the character you are pretending to be. You have to settle on who the person is, where you are, what you are doing, and why you are doing it. Although an improvisation is spontaneous, it is not without design, and you are obligated to contribute to that design as an actor by knowing the answers to the questions above. Improvisation is not all chance, although it is unrehearsed and unplanned. Perhaps you would like to work out some other improvisations for your fellow classmates to do.

The most common experiences of people who act are fear (commonly called stage fright), embarrassment, and self-consciousness. As you've probably discovered, you are no exception, and neither am I. But my purpose is not to make a professional actor out of you. Instead, I am interested in having you participate in acting situations so that you may attempt to unravel the mystery of characterization. Just as I have emphasized your need to know yourself, so must an actor know his character.

Every person is a variation on every other person. The more people you know, the more you know about people in general and yourself in particular. You can articulate some of that knowledge, and some of it you can only sense in a vague way. But we all act. Only some of us do it on a stage. Psychologists call it role playing. I would call it trying to get outside yourself in order to see inside.

Actors have to know every feeling a human being can experience. That is their business. Most of us experience a lot more than we ever realize. Acting helps us to discover those hidden feelings. In acting a role, take any line you have to say, and after that line write in the word that will describe the feeling the line articulates. For each line is an articulated feeling. Your character is the sum *plus* of those feelings. And that's what you are in your own life.

The world's a stage.

The play which you are about to read and perform has already been discussed in the chapter you just read. "String" is an adaptation by a twentieth-century playwright, Alice Childress, of a story by the nineteenth-century French short story writer Guy de Maupassant. The play was first performed by the Negro Ensemble Company in New York City in 1969 with an all-black cast.

THE PLAY'S THE THING

The play is about members of a block association. If you live in a large city, you may know about block associations. But if you live in a small town, as I do, you won't have much contact with such groups. A block association is made up of a group of neighbors in a large city who organize themselves as a small community in order to have a sense of a neighborhood and the possibility of political influence. If you wish, you can rewrite the play (remembering that Ms. Childress took all sorts of liberties with de Maupassant's short story). You might change the setting to a town meeting, a school picnic, a suburban party, or a family reunion. The dynamics are the same: an attempt is made to form a community out of a number of individuals, and the result is that a gentle man is abused by vulgarians.

Suit the action to the word.

In performing the play, be careful about the problem of the dialect. The purpose of dialect is to bring out the character, *not to make caricatures*. Dialect is like a localism: a sound or manner of speech becomes peculiar to a particular region or ethnic group—the midwestern twang, the southern drawl, the Scottish brogue, the New England broadness. Because it becomes an identifying feature of the group or locality, it is easily subject to ridicule and caricature. However, its existence has to do with convention, custom, and the history of language, and it should be respected as such. It takes a very skillful practitioner to do dialect well.

"String" takes place on a picnic ground during a picnic given by the Neighborhood Association. The cast consists of the following persons:

Mrs. Beverly, a neighborhood lady, very civic-minded
Mrs. Rogers, a neighborhood lady given to arrogant manners
Joe, a weird-o middle-aged character
Maydelle, a pleasant young woman
L. V. Craig, well-to-do owner of a bar and grill
Katy, a child

String

Time: *A Sunday summer morning.*
Place: *Near New York City.*
Scene: *An isolated spot of picnic ground . . . sparse grass, struggling bushes. A picnic table and benches, a tree stump, a large rock. The shadow of tall unseen trees shades the area. In the distance the sound of singing and laughter. Mrs. Beverly and Mrs. Rogers enter carrying picnic baskets, folding camp chairs, a blanket, a drink cooler, and other picnic items. Mrs. Rogers wears a simple, well-cut linen suit, spectator pumps, and a sun visor hat. Mrs. Beverly wears a splashy, colorful outfit . . . pants and top . . . and a large, fringed straw hat, loop earrings, and fancy high-heeled shoes. They are slightly breathless from running. Mrs. Beverly is laden down with most of the carried items—Mrs. Rogers subtly suggests that she has a servant in Mrs. Beverly.*

Mrs. Beverly: Yes, I am, I'm damn disgusted.
Mrs. Rogers: Use up the space. *(They hurriedly cover the table, rock and tree stump, benches, etc., with their possessions. Mrs. Rogers avoids work and grandly directs.)*

Mrs. Beverly: Oughta turn around and go right back home.

Mrs. Rogers: Now, there's no more room. Let 'em stay over there to themselves.

Mrs. Beverly: Mrs. Rogers.

Mrs. Rogers: Yes, Mrs. Beverly.

Mrs. Beverly: This is the last block association picnic I attend. This is it.

Mrs. Rogers: I'd say we need a new picnic chairlady.

Mrs. Beverly: Maydelle should be impeached . . . asked out. *(Loud laughter in the distance.)*

Mrs. Rogers: Loud, loud, loud . . . *too* loud. Oh, my God, here comes old Joe.

Mrs. Beverly: No.

Mrs. Rogers: *(Singing instructions to Mrs. Beverly.)* Let's be busy, busy, busy.

Mrs. Beverly: That man looks like he stinks.

Mrs. Rogers: Change, change, change the subject. I do like you in pink, Mrs. Beverly.

Mrs. Beverly: Thank you, Mrs. Rogers. *(Old Joe enters. He is about fifty-five but looks older than his years, wears odds and ends of cast-off clothing. Is rather apologetic and self-conscious about his appearance. His walk is apologetic and uncertain. He carries a much crumpled paper sack of lunch.)*

Joe: Well . . . er . . . mmmmm . . . er . . . nice day.

Mrs. Beverly: Beg pardon.

Joe: Er . . . well . . . I say . . . I say nice day.

Mrs. Rogers: So they tell me *(He tries to find a place to sit down but every possible spot has been covered by the ladies. He starts to move an item from the rock.)*

Mrs. Beverly: Don't move that.

Mrs. Rogers: She's going to sit there.

Joe: Well . . . on the rock?

Mrs. Beverly: *I* like to sit on rocks. *(He starts to move something from the tree stump.)*

Mrs. Rogers: And I like to sit on tree stumps.

Joe: Oh, well, who gon' sit on the chairs?

Mrs. Rogers: We're going to put the food on the chairs.

Joe: Then I guess I can sit on the table. Thassa joke. I was jokin'. I'll just stan' 'roun and watch.

Mrs. Rogers: Watch what?

Joe: Anything, whatever is goin' on. Pay me no mind.

Mrs. Rogers: Why don't you join the others? That's where the action is . . . as they say.

Joe: *They* tol' me the action was over here.

Mrs. Beverly: *(Tersely.)* Well, they lied. We just well might sit here and pray . . . just quietly pray and think about God and our souls and the beauty of nature . . . stuff like that.

Joe: Well, you mean y'all want me to move on?

Mrs. Beverly: I didn't say that. Why do people twist what you say? *(Maydelle enters.)*

Maydelle: Listen here, Mr. Joe, don't you pay L. V. any mind.

Joe: I ain't. What I care 'bout L. V. Craig? He get me today—that's all right, I get him tomorrow.

Mrs. Beverly: Hey, Maydelle. And how is our chairlady?

Maydelle: L. V. jokes and plays too rough. He told Joe to move on because he was scarin' the white folks away from the picnic area.

Mrs. Rogers: L. V. Craig is crude, cruel and crass, downright crass. But since L. V. Craig makes his living by running a third-rate bar and grill . . . what can one expect? Ohhh, but some of us are still trying to make a silk purse from a sow's ear . . . this block association is suddenly becoming overcrowded with the crass and the crude. L. V. Craig was drunk when he stepped off the bus. Who ever heard of arriving at an outing drunk? Drunk at eight in the morning?

Maydelle: He's not really drunk . . . just feelin' kind-a good.

Joe: Maydelle, I thank you for givin' me the free bus ticket but maybe I shouldn't-a come.

Mrs. Beverly: A *free* bus ticket?

Maydelle: It wasn't really free. Joe stuffed the circulars in the mail boxes.

Mrs. Beverly: Joe, when are you gonna spend some-a your money?

Joe: What money? I ain' got no money. Who say I got money?

Mrs. Beverly: They say that down there in that old basement room you got money sewed up in your mattress, all in the quilt . . .

Joe: Thassa lie. I ain't got no money . . . lyin' on me.

Mrs. Beverly: I hear you have seven or eight bank books.

Joe: Thassa lie. I ain' got no money . . . lyin' on me.

Mrs. Beverly: Buy yourself some clothes . . . spend it on you . . . you can't take it with you . . . no pockets in a shroud . . .

Joe: Ain' got it to spend.

Mrs. Beverly: If you don't spend that money, some heroin junkie is gonna break in there one night, beat your brains out and take it away from you and spend it up *for* you . . . now how good is that?

Joe: I ain' got no damn money.

Maydelle: Come on over under the big tree. Can't the block association sit together? Why can't we all sit together?

Mrs. Rogers: Might get shot at. All together someone may mistake us for a riot. Togetherness . . . sometimes I weary of togetherness. *(L. V. Craig enters waving a liquor bottle wrapped in a paper bag. He is very outgoing.)*

L. V. Craig: Hey, my man, don'tcha go away mad. The treat's on me. Drink up. It's free-for-nothin', kill yourself.

Joe: I don' drink.

L. V. Craig: Course not, you might have to buy one for somebody else sometime.

Mrs. Beverly: Maybe we should join the others. I got to sell these meat pies.

Mrs. Rogers: Sell what?

Mrs. Beverly: Meat pies. Fifty cents each. No ready ground meat, nothin' but chopped round.

Mrs. Rogers: Sell? You're going to sell things on a picnic?

L. V. Craig: You right, Miss Beverly, don' never give 'way the only thing you got to sell.

Mrs. Beverly: I gave them away last year . . . fifteen dollars worth of ground round . . . I gave it away.

Mrs. Rogers: They say the West Indians and the Jews are very much alike.

Mrs. Beverly: What kind of damn remark is that?

Maydelle: Oh, Mrs. Rogers, don't talk that way.

Mrs. Rogers: It's a compliment. Why are we so sensitive?

Mrs. Beverly: Making remarks——

Mrs. Rogers: I meant you were . . . clever.

Mrs. Beverly: I'm a widow. Everybody doesn't have a henpecked husband working in the Post Office.

Mrs. Rogers: I know many widows . . . and none of them are selling meat pies.

L. V. Craig: Hot-damn, hey Joe, you ain' even a successful miser. When somebody offer you somethin' free . . . take it.

Joe: I don' want your rot-gut whiskey . . . ol' rot-gut bar whiskey.

Maydelle: Let's not have an unpleasant day. Let's sing. Somebody pick a song.

Mrs. Rogers: In order to have a pleasant day you have to have people on the same level. This is an . . . an . . . an . . . ill-assorted group.

L. V. Craig: Here we go! Gotcha song for you. We shall overcome . . . We shall overcome . . .

Joe: *(Sincerely joins singing.)* We shall overcome some-da——y. Oh deep in my heart . . .

Maydelle: Oh shut up! Don't be funny, L. V.

Mrs. Rogers: This block association is bound to be ill-assorted because we have a block full of ill-assorted people.

L. V. Craig: Pick another song . . . 'nother song comin' up. Finger poppin' time. *(Pops out a rhythm.)* Beep beep, bo-peep; bang-bang-a-ring-a-lang, Oom, gowa black power, BLACK POWER!

Joe: Y'all gonna make trouble.

Mrs. Beverly: *(To Mrs. Rogers and the world in general.)* People in glass houses shouldn't throw stones and that goes for all of you. I can take the damn hot, crowded subway and get the hell on outta here, meat pies, BEACH UMBRELLA AND ALL!

Maydelle: Don't, don't do that.

Mrs. Beverly: It ain't like I don't have a home to go to.

L. V. Craig: All right, pretty mama, put that mess down. You goin' nowhere. I say so. Tell you what I'm gonna do, I'm gon' buy all the meat pies. Treat's on me. Whatcha got?

Mrs. Beverly: I made fifty.

Mrs. Rogers: *(To Maydelle.)* Mmmmm, a fast, cool twenty-five bucks.

Maydelle: Let it drop.

L. V. Craig: See if I got sump'n small here. Nothin' but one-yard and half-yard bills . . . I'll go getcha some chicken-feed change so I can lay twenty-five on you.

Mrs. Beverly: Pay me later, I know you good for it. Put your money away.

Mrs. Rogers: *(To Maydelle.)* He's always loaded . . . with money I mean.

L. V. Craig: Lay them meat pies on me. Live it up. *(As Mrs. Beverly opens the meat pies package she unwinds the string from around it, winds it up, and throws it on the ground. Joe notices it and watches his chance to pick it up when no one is noticing him.)*

Mrs. Rogers: That's good business . . . what you call public relations. He buys from you, then you go in his bar and grill and give him a little play . . . we all buy a bottle-a beer, the chicken in the basket. One hand washes the other.

Mrs. Beverly: *(To Maydelle as they pass out meat pies.)* She's on me. There is such a thing as jealousy.

Maydelle: Pay it no mind. *(Mrs. Rogers bites into a meat pie.)* I'll take a tray down to the others.

Mrs. Rogers: Dee-licious. They are good, they are too good. You should open a shop. Dee-licious. Two-a these and a green salad and you got your dinner. Could I take two or three home for Percy? He'll go mad. Dee-licious! Hey, L. V., why don't you put in a regular order for your bar and grill . . . you could use a few hundred-a these every week.

L. V. Craig: I sure could. Good!

Mrs. Rogers: Follow that up, Mrs. Beverly. He's interested in a regular order. Move on that, make your move, strike while the iron is hot.

Mrs. Beverly: *(Beaming.)* Thank you, dear-heart, help yourself. *(Joe quickly picks up the discarded string.)* What did you pick up, Joe?

Joe: Nothin', I didn't do nothin'.

L. V. Craig: *(As he sits on the rock, eating a pie.)* Be a man, will you? You don't have to scrounge 'round pickin' up stuff off the ground. The food is on the tray.

Joe: I ain' got no food. You leave me 'lone. I don' want none-a your free-ass food.

Maydelle: Oh, no, I'm sorry, we're not gonna have that kind of language.

Joe: *(Waving his paper sack.)* Don't gimmie nothin'. Mother may have and father may have but God bless the Black child that's got his own.

Maydelle: I'm surprised at you, surprised and disappointed.

L. V. Criag: We all know you got your own. But all I say is be a man.

Mrs. Beverly: What did you pick up?

Joe: Nothin.' None-a your business.

Mrs. Beverly: I saw you.

Joe: You did not.

Mrs. Rogers: Does it matter? Let's be big about it. Rise above the commonplace . . . rise above it all for just one day.

Joe: I don' ask nobody for nothin', I don't take nothin' and I didn't take no meat pie from the tray or off-a the ground or no place else.

L. V. Craig: Man, you just a damn liar.

Maydelle: It doesn't matter. Drop the subject.

Joe: I ain' took nothin', I say.

Mrs. Beverly: Joe, you're free to pick up what you please. I saw you, that's that, and that's the end of it.

Maydelle: Be kind . . . kindness goes a long way.

Joe: They been on me all day now . . . on the bus, off-a the bus. Leave off-a me. If I wasn't old, I'd knock you down, L. V. Yeah, I save a penny when I get hold-a one. I ain' got no family. If I don' put by somethin', who gonna do for me? One thing . . . I mind my business. Ain' got no friends, that's all right. A man's best friend ain' no dog . . . it's a dollar.

Mrs. Beverly: A truer word was never spoken.

L. V. Craig: If you bought somebody a bottle-a ale sometime, you might have a friend.

Joe: I'm a friend to everybody without any of 'em buyin' me no ale.

L. V. Craig: I can't stand cheapness. That's somethin' I don' even understand.

Joe: You understand stealin', cuttin' down your drinks . . . he puts water in the whiskey he sells.

L. V. Craig: How you know? You ever bought any? I'll bust you in your mouth.

Joe: I'm goin' off to sit to myself. You stay off-a me. You low down . . .

Maydelle: No more bad language. Doctor MacDonald is down there. Do you want him to hear you going on like that? Little children are down there . . . do you want them to hear you?

Joe: I'm goin' off by myself . . . not 'round nobody else.

L. V. Craig: Yeah, that's good, go on, I'm tired-a lookin' at you. *(Joe seems overwhelmed and almost about to cry. He clutches the sack to his bosom, turns and walks away and out of sight.)*

Maydelle: Joe . . . Joe . . .

L. V. Craig: Let him be. Didn't you hear him say he want to be to hisself?

Maydelle: Everybody does ride him. He is stingy, he is strange . . . but it's a sickness, a sickness in his mind. He doesn't hurt anybody. It's only a sickness.

Mrs. Beverly: It's a fact. Everybody torments the hell outta that poor old man, all of us.

L. V. Craig: Some people ask for that.

Mrs. Rogers: He's a sad case, very sad . . . depressing. One day they'll find him stretched out dead and the State of New York will grab hold-a whatever he's got stashed away in those mattresses. Oh, yes, the state will take over. Use the money to build another poorhouse. What you call poetic justice.

L. V. Craig: Talkin' 'bout I put water in the whiskey. Can you imagine that?

Maydelle: Yes, I can imagine it. I can imagine you doin' just 'bout anything.

L. V. Craig: (*Laughs.*) But I don't do much cryin' though. No cryin', no marchin', no prayin' . . . L. V. Craig's gon' git his if there's any gittin' to git. Pinchin' and prayin', scrimpin' and scufflin' . . . for somebody else not me . . . ain' for me. (*Mrs. Beverly wipes her eyes with handkerchief.*)

Maydelle: What's the matter?

Mrs. Beverly: I can't blame him too much. It's hard for our people to accumulate anything. Hard to even just make it. What have I got to show for my whole life? A tray of meat pies. Old age is not to be laughed at. The only way to save anything is to do without. God help the day I can't do for myself.

Mrs. Rogers: Oh, don't worry . . . there's always welfare.

Mrs. Beverly: All my life I been doin', goin', workin', makin' my own way. Do I own my own home someplace, huh? Old Joe is a little wise even in his folly. He's a wise old fool.

Maydelle: Our people do see a hard way but I can't go along with that doin' without. Joe buys half-rotten vegetables . . . saves old boxes and newspaper . . . the janitors give him the papers for helping them pull garbage . . . Mr. Rutledge lets him sleep in the basement . . . who can live like that?

L. V. Craig: The hell with old age. You got today, use that. Fly high while you flyin.' When it's gone, go on down to skid row and drink canned heat with the winos.

Mrs. Rogers: Well, let's eat, drink, and be merry 'cause tomorrow we gonna catch hell.

L. V. Craig: (*Laughs.*) There you go.

Maydelle: Talk 'bout age . . . not soundin' on anybody but I'm the youngest one here. You folks get another chairlady 'cause I'm gonna spend some time with my little boy. I'm goin' to night school. I got a full time job and that's more than a handful. I'm sick-a tryin' to keep peace and do work for the community . . . it's not appreciated.

Mrs. Rogers: That's not true. Who could do the job you're doing? You couldn't be replaced.

Mrs. Beverly: You're marvelous . . . and so much patience. *(Joe wanders back in and sits to one side.)* Come on, old timer, there's enough for everybody.

Joe: No, thank you. *(Opens the bag and takes out what looks like a mashed piece of bread.)*

L. V. Craig: Doggone, what the hell is that you eatin'? The heel of the bread . . . the end-a the bread.

Maydelle: Behave, L. V.

Joe: I ain' botherin' a soul. I'm just sittin' here watchin'.

L. V. Craig: Cause watchin' is free.

Maydelle: *(Throws a paper cup at L. V.'s head.)* I told you.

L. V. Craig: Oh, beat me, baby. See, she's sweet on me . . . What you gon' throw next, baby? That's a down-home chick. *(Offstage record player renders rock and roll.)* Come on, Maydelle . . . little Boog-a-loo.

Maydelle: I don't do all that.

Mrs. Beverly: I do. *(They dance . . . all join in except Joe. Mrs. Beverly forces him to his feet.)* Come on, shake somethin' . . . shake it up for the block association. *(They form a circle and dance around Joe. Maydelle and Joe dance. He begins to enjoy himself with abandon.)* Don't wait! Do your dancin' now!

L. V. Craig: What the hell . . . damn . . . cut the noise . . . I been robbed. My wallet is gone . . . four and a half yards . . . four hundred and fifty dollars gone . . . I swear . . . no kiddin' . . . it's gone.

Mrs. Beverly: Oh, dear God, and there goes my meat pies right down everybody's throat.

L. V. Craig: Hell with meat pies. My money's gone.

Mrs. Beverly: Sometimes I wonder what God is doing.

L. V. Craig: Everybody stay where you at. My roll is gone.

Maydelle: Now wait, don't stir up all that noise. Are any of us thieves?

Mrs. Beverly: I haven't a thing to hide. Search me, in fact I'll search myself and my belongings . . . the important thing is to get L. V.'s money.

Mrs. Rogers: Nobody's gonna search my person. That's unconstitutional . . . an invasion of privacy.

Mrs. Beverly: I don't have anything to hide.

Mrs. Rogers: I don't have anything to hide either. I wish to go on record as protesting any searching as an unconstitutional procedure . . .

L. V. Craig: Everybody's so friggin' honest 'til my money's gone. Where's my wallet? Where's my damn billfold?

Maydelle: Be calm. Now, let's just be quiet for a minute.

Mrs. Rogers: She's right. Keep still!

Mrs. Beverly: Don't you raise your voice to me.

Maydelle: In the first place why say it was *stolen*? Do we know it has been stolen? No.

L. V. Craig: Got-dog. Look-a here . . . *(Turns his pockets inside out.)* It's gone . . . find my billfold. Find it or I'll call the law.

Mrs. Beverly: We can see it's gone. I'm with you, L. V. I'm a witness . . . it's gone.

Mrs. Rogers: It may be at home or in the Be-bop Bar and Grill.

Joe: *(To himself.)* There you go, it's at home.

L. V. Craig: How the hell it's gonna be home when I took it out to pay for the meat pies . . . didn't have any small money and I put it back in my pocket . . .

Mrs. Beverly: That's a fact . . . everybody knows that.

Mrs. Rogers: Why would anyone bring four hundred and fifty cash dollars on a picnic? Why?

L. V. Craig: Cause it's mine and I can take it where I please . . . my rent money . . . Cadillac payment . . . I cleaned out my cash drawer . . . all-a these hold ups . . . gotta explain why I got my own money.

Maydelle: Yeah, but don't say it's stolen. Maybe you dropped it. *(Joe is busy searching for the money under the table, etc.)* Look everywhere . . . in the grass . . . along the path . . . *(They all search but Mrs. Rogers gives a rather lackluster peep here and there.)*

Mrs. Rogers: I don't see anything. It's gone. Just kiss it good-by.

Mrs. Beverly: Rent money . . . that's awful.

Joe: You should never carry so much. Suppose somebody backs you into a alley and hold you up? It happens . . . And how 'bout these self-service elevator things? I never ride the self-service. I walk.

Mrs. Beverly: If you live in the basement, I guess you don't have to.
Joe: It goes down to the basement too.
Mrs. Beverly: I suppose.
Joe: But I walk . . . walk and don't carry any money.
Maydelle: What color was the wallet?
L. V. Craig: Did you find one of any color? Askin' foolish questions.
Mrs. Rogers: It's not here.
Mrs. Beverly: Nowhere to be found.
Maydelle: Not there.
Mrs. Rogers: Hold it. Stop. Everybody stop. Do you remember when we were teasing Joe?
L. V. Craig: Never mind the memories. I want my money.
Maydelle: Joe, help us to look.
Joe: If it ain' here, I don't know where to look.
Mrs. Rogers: Joe, what did you pick up from the ground? What did you hide in your pocket?
L. V. Craig: Yeah, you did pick up somethin'. And I said don't pick up stuff off-a the ground.
Mrs. Beverly: And I recall you sayin' it. Your very words. You sure did.
L. V. Craig: Listen here . . . everybody turn their back and I'm gon count to five . . . when we turn 'round let the wallet be right there in the middle-a the circle . . . then we forget the whole business and no more said . . . turn! *(Everybody turns while L. V. Craig counts.)* One-two-three—*(Much peeping going on as L. V. Craig counts. Only Joe refuses to turn and take part.)* four . . . *(L. V. Craig spins around to catch the culprit.)* Five dammit! That's fair enough. *(To Joe.)* You the only one playin' it cool 'cause you know what the hell it's all about. You picked up my billfold, I saw you.
Joe: ME? You crazy.
L. V. Craig: Yeah, I am. Tell you jus' how crazy. I'm gon' offer a reward for the return-a my wallet. Give it to you or anybody else . . . fifty dollars, no questions asked. Everybody spread out and give one more look, then Joe can hand it back and get the fifty dollars.
Joe: Don't you talk to me that-a way. You ain' big enough to bandy my name like that. I'm a honor-ful person. I got honor, I ain' picked up nothin'.
Mrs. Beverly: But everybody here saw you pick up something.

L. V. Craig: Hand it over, Joe. I ain' gon' hit you, you too old to hit. And I ain't gon' call the cop . . . everybody hear me give my word, so you jus' hand it to me.

Mrs. Rogers: That's fair enough, very fair.

Joe: I ain' never stole nothin' in my whole life.

Mrs. Beverly: Mr. Rutledge caught you coming outta the basement with a box.

Joe: Yeah, full of magazines. Somebody threw 'em out on the dumbwaiter. That's garbage . . . garbage belong to anybody.

Maydelle: He didn't take anything, L. V., Joe doesn't steal.

Joe: Thank you, mam, Maydelle. Search me. *(He rips off his coat and reveals a tattered but clean shirt. Turns out the ragged pockets of the coat. Steps out of his shoes. His socks have holes in the toes.)* Nothin' . . . nothin' . . . nothin' . . .

Mrs. Rogers: He is as raggedy as a bowl-a sauerkraut.

L. V. Craig: Don't show me no pockets. You went away, you had time to hide it. Where you put it?

Mrs. Beverly: You did go away, then you came back.

Joe: He chased me . . . yall was on me . . . L. V. was at me and I was afraid . . . Yeah, I was . . . swear to God, then I went away and . . . that's why.

L. V. Craig: Aw, don' hand me that. If you was so scared, what you come back for? *(All show off their T.V. knowledge about crime.)*

Mrs. Beverly: Good question. Why *did* you come back?

Mrs. Rogers: But you don't have to answer him. Remember his civil rights.

L. V. Craig: Why the hell you go 'way and then come back?

Mrs. Rogers: *(Enjoying the situation, talking down to him.)* First he must be warned. Joe, you should know that anything you say may be held against you. You can refuse to say anything without the advice of your lawyer.

Joe: I don' need no lawyer, I ain't done nothin'. You chased me . . . I was afraid . . .

L. V. Craig: Why did you come back?

Joe: Them others down there they was kinda chasin' me too.

Mrs. Beverly: Kinda chasin' you? Did they chase you or didn't they?

Joe: You know . . . I mean like they was givin' me the cold shoulder.

Mrs. Beverly: No, I don't know.

L. V. Craig: All right, you was scared-a me . . . so what you come back for?

Joe: I thought you had forgot 'bout . . . that you had forgot . . .

L. V. Craig: Forgot 'bout the wallet?

Joe: No, not forgot about the green wallet . . .

L. V. Craig: Man, how you know what color it is?

Joe: You had it in your hand when you was countin' through all-a your money, that's when I saw the color.

Mrs. Rogers: I didn't even notice the color.

Mrs. Beverly: We saw you pick it up.

Maydelle: Oh, Joe. You did pick up something. What was it?

Joe: It wasn't a wallet . . . so what's the difference?

Mrs. Beverly: We want to get to the bottom of this.

Maydelle: It would help to clear the air.

Joe: Must I tell? I don't want to tell it.

Maydelle: You don't have to . . . but I'd like you to clear yourself.

Joe: *(Takes the piece of string from his pocket and unwinds it.)* It was . . . it was a piece-a string. I picked up this piece-a string.

L. V. Craig: You must think you talkin' to a lamb. You was lookin' on the ground afterward like tryin' to see if any damn money had dropped out.

Joe: All-a yall . . . search me . . . call the cop . . . but don' do what you doin' to me. Down home . . . down home is where my mama's grave is but I swear on her grave, 'fore God . . . I ain' never been arrested in all-a my years.

L. V. Craig: A piece-a string. Ain' this a cryin' shame?

Mrs. Rogers: Let me see it. It's not long enough to really tie anything. What were you going to do with it?

Joe: I don' know. It was there 'cause she threw it away.

Mrs. Beverly: I don't throw trash around.

Joe: It's only a piece-a string.

L. V. Craig: Okay, old-timer, have it your way. You gon' stand up tellin' a bareface lie . . . I'm gonna have you picked up by the cop.

Mrs. Rogers: I beg your pardon. What can the cop do? You must have the evidence?

Joe: Maydelle, everybody . . . look-a me here. I was standin' here . . . I saw her with the piece-a string . . . she throwed it down . . .

Mrs. Beverly: I'm on the clean-up committee of the block association . . . why would I throw trash on the ground? This year I have handed out thirty . . . KEEP NEW YORK CITY CLEAN signs . . . *"Every litter bit hurts."* . . . So why would I . . .

Joe: But you did . . . you throwed it down . . . I waited 'til nobody was payin' me any mind . . . then I stooped down . . . look, look-a me here . . . this how I did . . . I stooped down and picked it up like so . . .

L. V. Craig: And when you saw me watchin' you, you bent over and hid it in your coat. Now why is that?

Joe: I . . . I guess . . . I . . . oh, I don' know.

L. V. Craig: When I ask what it was, you said it was none-a my affair. All that to-do 'bout a piece-a string?

Mrs. Beverly: He did say it was none-a your business. We heard that much.

Joe: If I was to burn in hell forever . . . if God was to strike me dead . . .

Maydelle: Listen, Joe, don't worry yourself this way. I know you didn't do it, know it like I know my own name.

Joe: Thank you, ma'am, I thank you. I ain' scared-a police . . . but I don' want my name bandyin' roun' 'bout stealin' . . . God be my judge.

Maydelle: But it must be found. We can't be sure it's gone until we search everywhere. Who knows, maybe it was jus' the string. No one saw him with a wallet.

L. V. Craig: That ain' even a good lie. A piece-a string.

Joe: I would never do nothin' like no stealin' . . . what I got I get by the sweat-a my brow . . . I don't even beg . . . don't even get no help like the welfare or the old age . . . how come you don' 'cuse somebody else 'sides me . . . why you say me? If I found it, I'd-a turn it in. What I picked up was string . . . Look-a me here, I was standin' on this spot, right there . . . then the others . . . somebody was over by the tree.

Maydelle: I know it. Joe wouldn't do anything like that. Maybe you lost it on the road . . . search down the road. . . .

L. V. Craig: Jus' wastin' everybody's damn time. *(Snatches the string and holds it up.)* I oughta choke him with it. String.

Maydelle: We're gonna make a good, thorough search . . .

Mrs. Rogers: Just to think, my club is giving a beautiful boatride and fashion show today . . . and I got myself caught in this trap.

Maydelle: I was goin' to the fresh-air fund camp . . . to see my boy.

Mrs. Beverly: I was up cooking all night long, that's what I been doing.

Mrs. Rogers: It's all right. L. V. has cheated the hell outta everybody in the neighborhood. You can't steal from a thief.

Mrs. Beverly: Talkin' 'bout me throwin' stuff on the ground.

Maydelle: Listen . . . don't spread this kind of talk all over the picnic grounds. It's a reflection on the block association, a reflection on the picnic, and a reflection on the race. No one stole any money. We'll simply find it. Don't worry, Joe, we'll clear you by finding it.

Joe: Clear me? How you gon' clear me? I didn't do nothin'!

L. V. Craig: Give me my money in my hand, I'm going to knock your teeth down your lyin' throat. *(L. V. Craig grabs Joe and almost lifts him off the ground . . . he shakes him. The women scream . . . they separate them and pull L. V. Craig offstage.)*

Maydelle: Do it and I'll throw a picket line around that bar and grill and put you out of business. You gonna commit murder over a few damn dollars?

Mrs. Rogers: *(Enjoying the excitement.)* Well, this is where the action is. All this on account of some string. *(Winks at Joe.)* Piece-a string, right? *(They scatter and look for the wallet.)*

Maydelle: Come on, search everybody, search everywhere.

Mrs. Beverly: For your sake I hope it was string . . . although I didn't throw anything on the ground.

Joe: *(Calls after them.)* When you find it . . . don't beg my pardon . . . don't 'pologize . . . yall gon be sorry . . . damn your soul, L. V. Craig, I ain' scared-a you . . . you can kill me dead but you can't put no bad mouth on me . . . can't make no thief outta me . . . ha-ha . . . hell with you . . . hell with all-a you . . . *(Searches under the table . . . glances through things on the table, etc.)* Why should I look for it . . . they too ungrateful . . . if I find it they'll say I had it all the time . . . hell with lookin' . . . why should I be lookin' . . . puttin' on airs folk . . . that's who got it . . . *(Slaps his hands together and determines to forget the whole affair . . . desperately . . . He turns on a transistor radio.)* Hell with you. I'm gon' enjoy myself. I should worry I should care . . .

Radio Commentator: Your news around the clock . . . six planes were downed in Vietnam today . . . Vietnam . . . enemy dead . . . North Vietnam and South Vietnam . . . the Vietnamese . . . Saigon . . . China . . . Hai-phong . . . three miles to the North . . . from China . . . internal strife . . . the hawks and the doves . . . senators . . . congressmen, the President . . . the far left and the liberals . . . also the black power advocates and the responsible Negro leaders . . . third party is lined up—The Black Panthers . . . Mayor Lindsay . . . declares Afro-American day . . . tomorrow is Whitey day . . . Whitey Ford day . . . the great sportsman . . . and the Olympics and the controversy concerning De Gaulle . . . Expo 67 . . . Detroit is burning . . . that's Detroit, Newark and all points west . . . the poverty program and the investigation . . . all excessive bail . . . Stokely Carmichael . . . Governor Wallace . . . the Pope . . . Rap Brown . . . and the New Orleans Mystery moves forward . . . who assassinated . . . for it was Marcus Garvey who first . . . the Dubois clubs . . . *(Joe is so distracted that he pops his fingers and keeps time to unheard music . . . doesn't realize he's listening to news.)*

Joe: Hell, what I care 'bout L. V. and them damn trouble-makin' niggers? *(He dances to imaginary music.)* Yeah, shake it up, what I care? Oh, play that thing . . . Play that music.

Radio Commentator: *(Voice down lower.)* The elderly woman and her three friends were found murdered the search goes on and the poverty program taxes 10 percent in order to share the cost of outer space and birth control and abortion controversy study is being conducted by the Ford Foundation and all points south . . . flood in Alaska and the Bedford Stuyvesant area is quiet . . . Haryou Act and school strike program with the teachers and school lockout. . . .

Joe: What I care? I bet it's one-a them uppity ones. *(He decides to look in their purses to see if they have the money. He looks in Mrs. Beverly's bag . . .)* Jus' 'cause they be dressed up don't mean they can't be guilty too . . . sure, they *could* be guilty. *(Maydelle enters while Joe has his hand down in the handbag.)*

Radio Commentator: Another cutback in the program and the riots continue with Dow Jones up Universal Steel down to the moon rocket soft landing with Tel-star life sentence draft card burning . . .

Joe: *(With one hand down in the purse he pops the fingers of the other.)* I . . . I was listenin' to Dizzy Gillespie and . . . shakin' it up for . . . dancin' . . . livin' for today and the block committee . . . *(Maydelle turns off the radio.)* I was searchin' to see if somebody else stole it . . . that's what.

Maydelle: Joe, maybe you're sick.

Joe: No, I ain't. I thought one-a them mighta took it. After all they 'cusin' me.

Maydelle: *(Takes the bag away from him, looks in it and finds the contents intact.)* Joe, I believe you, I always believe you. No matter how things look . . . for some reason I believe in you.

Joe: Thank you, ma'am, Maydelle.

Maydelle: But don't do anything else, just stop.

Joe: But I ain' done nothin'. I told you it was a piece-a string.

Maydelle: Not that . . . I mean don't do anything at all. You're what you call low man on the totem pole. The cards are stacked against you.

Joe: I'm goin' on home that's what I'm gon' do.

Maydelle: No, you can't. That would look like you ran away with the money.

Joe: I could go down near the beach and ask if they got a lost and found . . . see if somebody turned in four hundred and fifty dollars . . .

Maydelle: No, don't do that . . . you mustn't . . . every move you make is suspect.

Joe: *(Worried.)* I oughta bust L. V. in his mouth . . . even if he kills me . . . I oughta fight him even if I lose . . . it's my honor . . . I'm so proud of my honor. That's all I got, my honor.

Maydelle: *(Firmly.)* You are too stubborn and hardheaded. You have to conduct yourself in such a manner that you will gain allies for your cause.

Joe: My cause?

Maydelle: You want your name cleared?

Joe: I guess so but I ain' done nothin'.

Maydelle: Joe, you can't live in this world all alone. You're powerless to go it by yourself. Now, I can't intercede for you if you keep . . . keep on . . .

Joe: Keep on what?

Maydelle: Doing whatever you do to make things seem the way they seem. Oh, look at you. If you had a nice suit, perhaps none of this would have happened.

Joe: L. V. got a nice suit, he got maybe forty nice suits and he live in a pretty white house with a lawn in front of it . . . but he cheats . . . he puts water in the whiskey . . . that's stealin' . . . thou shalt not covet . . .

Maydelle: But he doesn't look like a thief, and that's very important.

Joe: What does a thief look like?

Maydelle: If you don't try to change your ways and be a little like other people, it's going to go very hard for you. After all, they can't do all the changing in order to accommodate you. Why can't you realize that?

Joe: Maydelle, I don't believe yall treat me right . . . seem like yall pickin' on me all the time. Not you cause like you say . . . you for me . . . but all-a the others . . . can't you tell 'em real plain how I am and explain me clear?

Maydelle: I try. But you have to do your part too. It's so easy to blame our hardships on others. I know how they are . . . they're not nice, but it's their block . . . it's yours too, but not as much. You're just as good as they are. Show 'em.

Joe: I'm better than they are. Didn't you just say they're not nice? Bible say love one another. They don't love nobody, not even themselves much less each other.

Maydelle: Joe, Joe, Joe . . .

Joe: That L. V. is no good. He shot a man one time, shot and killed him dead right in the Be-bop Bar and Grill . . . fella fell dead right cross a platter ful-a barbecue ribs.

Maydelle: The fella was tryin' to hold him up. L. V. was protectin' his property.

Joe: He don' do right but everybody like him.

Maydelle: We don't like him but he's a good sport . . . he hands out a lotta treats.

Joe: Yeah . . . well, but . . .

Maydelle: But what?

Joe: Nothin'. It was a piece-a string.

Maydelle: You stop thrashin' around and doin'. Don't be so busy. Be quiet, the quieter the better . . . then they'll see by your manner. Do you want to frighten people all the time?

Joe: No, ma'am. They scared a me?

Maydelle: Be quiet, be good, and I'll do what I can with the others. Maybe we'll find the billfold and go home unified. A house divided . . .

Joe: A house divided cannot stand. Do not divide the house.

Maydelle: Sit there and be quiet. Take no more action on your own. You only make enemies . . . and you'll be the loser. Quiet.

Joe: Yes'm. Next week I'm going to buy me a nice suit. Right? *(Maydelle goes off to join the search. Joe starts to turn on the radio but draws back his hand in time.)* Don't do nothin' . . . no house-dividin'. *(A little girl enters skipping rope.)*

Katy: A lollypop stick makes me sick
A wigga-waggle wigga-waggle
Two, four, six
(She decides to tease Joe.)
Yah, yah, Joe-Joe, Yah, yah, Joe-Joe . . .
Joe: Go 'way, Katie, I got no time to play with you.
Katy: Yell at me . . . chase me.
Joe: Not today. I got to be quiet. My soul is sick.
Katy: Aw, what's the matter?
Joe: Disgrace. I'm dyin' from disgrace.
Katy: *(Worried about his grief)* I'm sorry I hurt your feelings, Joe, I'm sorry.
Joe: Go 'way and leave me alone. It was a piece-a string . . . that's all . . . *(Screams at her.)* Why the hell did I pick it up!
Katy: You're scarin' me.
Joe: I'm sorry. Don't be scared. Here a penny for you. *(She takes the penny.)* Now be a nice little girl and go play someplace else. *(Katy skips behind the tree stump and stumbles on Craig's wallet.)*
Katy: Joe, is this your wallet?
Joe: What? What you say?
Katy: *(Holds out the purse.)* Is this yours?
Joe: Praise God. Open it, open it . . . see if there's money inside . . . praise God . . . there it is . . . looka that money. Ain't that a pretty sight? You got to give it to L. V. Craig, the owner of the Be-bob Bar and Grill.
Katy: *(Gives the purse to him.)* You give it to him. I gotta go. Tomorrow I'm goin' on a trip . . . Aunt Susie's in North Carolina . . . we're gonna be on a train . . . and goin' swimmin' . . .
Joe: *(Flinching as though the wallet burns his hands.)* No, that's no good . . . I gotta be quiet . . . It's just that . . . well, I can't make no move. Don't go. Please, Katy, don't go. I'll call 'em back and you gon' have-ta tell 'em how you found it by the tree stump . . . then you gotta give it to L. V. . . . and clear my name.
Katy: *(A little uncomfortable.)* I gotta go back to my mama.
Joe: *(Holds her by the arm and places the wallet in her hand.)* Wait, wait. You hold it now. *(Katy is tugging to escape.)* Hey . . . hey there, yall! . . . *(He whistles.)* . . . Maydelle! Hey, L. V.! Come back! It's found! Come on back here. *(Katy begins to whimper.)*
Maydelle: What is it?
Mrs. Beverly: You found it? *(Mrs. Rogers, L. V. Craig enter.)*

Joe: *(Almost hysterical.)* There, look-a there . . . there, there you go. The wallet is in her hand. All the money . . . look-a there . . . Katy found it.

L. V.: *(Takes the wallet.)* It sure is there . . . all there. Where you find it, sugar pie?

Katy: *(Sniffling.)* Under the tree.

Voice: *(Offstage.)* Katy.

Mrs. Rogers: Girl, your mama is lookin' for you.

Mrs. Beverly: That is the damndest thing. I looked under the tree, and I didn't see it.

Katy: I have to go, Joe told me to give it to you and tell how I found it.

L. V. Craig: Yeah, how 'bout that? Soon's you leave him alone . . . the billfold turns up.

Mrs. Beverly: I, for one, am sure glad you found it. *(Starts passing meat pies.)*

L. V. Craig: You a rascal from the word go. But it's good you returned it.

Joe: *(Grabs Katy as she is about to leave.)* It was under the tree. Katy, tell 'em.

Katy: I told him! I told him! You're hurting my arm again. Please, Joe, don't hurt it any more. Let me go home. I did what you said.

L. V. Craig: Turn that baby's arm loose . . . I say turn her loose . . . or I'll knock you down.

Katy: And I don't want your old penny! *(Gives penny to Joe.)*

Maydelle: Let go, Joe. *(He releases Katy.)* Run along, Katy. *(Katy runs away.)*

L. V. Craig: You took it, put it back, then got the child to turn it in.

Joe: Please don't lie on me no more. All this lyin' is hurtin' me . . . don't nobody wanta be under a cloud on accounta lyin'. How you like somebody to do you that away? Do unto others like you want for yourself. It was a piece-a string I found . . . nothin' but string. The child . . . Katy found the wallet . . . and I told her to give it back 'cause I didn't want it to look like . . .

L. V. Craig: Oh, calm yourself, man . . . you makin' yourself sick. No harm done. Whatever you did, however you did it . . . I forgive you. Hell with it . . . my money is back . . . and that's the end of it.

Mrs. Rogers: Temptation . . . temptation is around us all the time . . . but God gave this man a conscience.

Mrs. Beverly: So let's stop talking about it. It's over.

Mrs. Rogers: It's a block association picnic and we should all sit together . . . looks so some-timey to be off this way. Everybody hold on to their belongings . . . purses, wallets, whatever . . . *(They are gathering belongings. She gives an aside to Mrs. Beverly.)* Wasn't that a fast one?

L. V. Craig: *(Laughs.)* You know one thing, man? Now that I got my bread back . . . I tell you this much. If I took somethin', I sure in hell would keep it. Don't never chicken out! Big enough to do it . . . go on and see it through. You sure ain' no thief . . . you jus' a rascal.

Maydelle: It's Mrs. Johnson's birthday and they're about to cut the cake. Let's go and have some of the cake . . . home-made cake . . .

Mrs. Rogers: Oh, she does bake beautiful cakes.

Mrs. Beverly: *(Bursts out laughing.)* A piece of string . . . that I threw on the ground . . . and me a member of the clean-up committee.

Joe: The wallet has been found and Katy found it.

L. V. Craig: Aw, shut-up your damn mouth. We got a double-pronged action goin' for us 'round here. One finds and the other reports. One is a full-grown, rusty man . . . the other is a baby child. Tell it any way you want but you mixed up in it.

Mrs. Rogers: *(Aside to Mrs. Beverly.)* Let's have a little fun.

Mrs. Beverly: Oh, now, leave him alone.

Mrs. Rogers: How did it happen? About the string I mean . . . Joe, how did it go down?

Joe: I was standing there when I saw the string.

Mrs. Rogers: That's right . . . and where was I?

Joe: You were where you at.

L. V. Craig: I do recall that. But how 'bout the money . . . the money bein' found . . . *(Offstage the birthday song, "Happy Birthday to You." The song continues through to end of play.)*

Joe: Over by the tree . . . the child and the . . . the piece of string.

L. V. Craig: Now don' get confused. Keep your story straight. You'd-a done better to keep dat money. *(They all laugh, except Maydelle.)*

Mrs. Beverly: In the middle-a your rejoicin' don' forget to pay me for the meat pies before you start missin' your bankroll again.

L. V. Craig: Have no fear, L. V. is here . . . if I run outta money, I'll pay you off with a piece-a string!

Joe: On my mother's grave, if I die tomorrow . . . call the child back. Katy . . . hey, Katy . . . Katy . . . Katy . . . *(Runs to the tree.)* Bet there's some kinda mark here on the ground . . . see how high the grass is here? . . . and there's the rock . . . maybe it was behind the rock and got kicked over to . . .

Mrs. Rogers: Yes, we know. (*All leave carrying the picnic things. Mrs. Beverly lingers behind.*)

Joe: (*To Mrs. Beverly.*) You know how it was. Don'tcha believe me? I didn't do it.

Mrs. Beverly: Mister, I don't judge a soul, not a damn soul. I'm not laughin' at you. Old age is one hell-of-a-time. God forgive me the thought . . . but I'm not too sure I would have returned it. Knowin' L. V. got more where that came from, I'm afraid to say just what I would have done. You did well and it's all over.

Joe: Don't say that to me, don't go 'way thinkin' that. It was right there for anyone to see . . . string! Just string!

Mrs. Beverly: Come get yourself some cake . . . have some fun. It's all over, no harm done. I don't blame you. (*She follows the others. There is a moment of strained silence between Joe and Maydelle.*)

Joe: It was . . . it was string. Maydelle . . . don't you know truth when you hear it . . . truth . . . you'n me, we know that, huh?

Maydelle: I'm proud of you . . .

Joe: Thank you, ma'am, Maydelle, thank you. You for me like you say . . .

Maydelle: I'm proud and glad you gave it back. You've justified my faith . . . I'm proud because you couldn't steal. You just couldn't . . . even if you wanted to . . . you couldn't . . .

Joe: (*Grabs a thermos bottle from the table.*) I'll beat your damn brains out! Say you believe me! Say it or I'll kill you . . .

Maydelle: Put that down . . . please, put it down . . .

Joe: Say you believe it was string . . . say it! (*Offstage crowd laughter and birthday song now set to rock and roll beat.*)

Maydelle: Please, for my sake . . . put it down . . . it's all right . . .

Joe: I say . . . say you believe it!

Maydelle: I believe you . . . I believe it was string . . . a piece of string . . . there! It was string. And don't you ever speak to me again for as long as you live. (*She exits. He is alone.*)

Joe: String . . . string . . . a piece-a string . . . it was a piece-a string . . . string . . . string . . . a piece-a string . . . (*Slumps to the ground. Lights dim.*)

CURTAIN

What is the question?

The only conclusion is no conclusion. A statement like that may confuse you, or even make you angry. I present it as the fitting close to this book, but not because I am mean. I do want you to be steeped in contradictions such as "In the end is the beginning." I want you to be submerged by the contraries, paradoxes, and ambiguities you encounter in your life. I want you to think of questions, not answers. I want you to finish this book intent upon problems, not solutions.

THERE IS NO CONCLUSION

This book was not written as a how-to-make-a-speech book nor as a how-to-talk-to-your-neighbor book. You know how to talk, and you knew about making a speech before you opened the book. Rather, this book was written in my hope of opening your curiosity and imagination to the pleasure and pain of talking, of verbal exchange between people. Speechmaking is a formal means of talking, just as debate is a formal means of disagreement. The way to the formal is through the informal.

Contrary to the popular lament that communication is no longer possible, I say communication is not only possible, necessary, and essential, but also natural. Everything is falsehood but silence, and silence is unbearable. We therefore *have* to talk. Think about that statement. I believe that we should stop complaining about what we cannot communicate to each other and, instead, devote some time and diligence to finding out what we *can* say to each other. The problem is to find out what each of us has to say. It is to that problem that this book has been directed.

In the beginning was the Word.

If you have something to say, it matters how you say it. I know that each of you has something to talk about. That's why I want you to learn how to say it well. The closer you can get to the feeling you wish to communicate, the more beautiful, efficient, and inspiring your expression will be. Beautiful communication is equally pleasing to the speaker and the listener. It takes searching, effort, energy, persistence, courage, nagging, desire, and self-respect to learn to talk well.

I have asked you to respect your fingerprints and voiceprints and those of your neighbor. I have asked you to seek out your individuality. I have asked you to tolerate, if not respect, your feelings about everything. I have said to you that your identity—your personal definition of yourself—can be illuminated by the words you utter. Those words are articulated feelings. I have asked you to search for those feelings and to go out and get information and evidence to support the thoughts, ideas, and opinions that you already have. The reason there is no conclusion is that there is no conclusion to you.

"Do you know who you're talking to?" Has that question ever been asked of you? Have you ever asked that question of someone? If you hear that question differently now that you have finished this book, I will consider the book a success. The fact is that you are always in the process of becoming. You and I are never fixed or constant. We are neither courageous nor cowardly, but we are both courageous and cowardly. We are neither loyal nor disloyal, but both; neither faithful nor unfaithful, but both. You and I are not criminals, but we are capable of committing a crime.

None of us know how we will behave in the next situation we encounter in life, although we have much past evidence that gives clues to the behavior we might expect. The world, nevertheless, is a sudden place. No matter how much we prepare to behave in a certain way, we are never sure of the outcome. Let me tell you two stories from literature about men who thought they could prepare for their future behavior.

Jim, in Joseph Conrad's novel *Lord Jim*, is a sailor who anticipates an emergency on board his ship—a shipwreck or some such event in which he will be called on to be courageous, generous, and helpful.

That time comes, but instead of acting heroically, Jim jumps off the ship and saves himself, abandoning the passengers to fend for themselves. That is not what he expected to do by any means but, when the situation arose, his fear, his sense of self-survival, and his cowardice contributed to his action. Have you known such a situation in your own life, even if considerably less dramatic?

Another story of the irrational taking over in time of crisis is Eugene O'Neill's play *The Emperor Jones.* Brutus Jones has fled to a West Indian island after trouble with the police in the United States. On the island, he becomes the emperor of an entire community, but he anticipates the day when he will be discovered to be a former railroad porter, not a divine chieftan, as the natives think him to be. To prepare for that day, he has devised a scheme to escape, has hidden food, and has planned his getaway. When the fateful day does indeed arrive and Jones's life is being sought by the natives, he begins to put his plan into action. But fear takes over and he can't find the escape route, and he can't locate the food. He goes right around in a circle until he ends up in the hands of the natives who are seeking his death.

I use those stories as illustrations about rational and strong persons who, in anticipating their behavior, never took into account their feelings—those irrational impulses that eventually were to be the determining forces in their fates. Knowing about your feelings cannot safeguard you against the dangers of the next event in your life. However, it might provide you with the margin of safety that the Irish playwright Synge described when writing about the fishermen of the Aran Islands: those who are afraid of the sea only get drowned now and again, but those who aren't afraid get drowned all the time. The Bible puts it differently: "The fear of the Lord is the beginning of knowledge."

In this book, Dustin Hoffman, Kurt Vonnegut, Jr., and I have encouraged you to be in touch with your feelings. But that is not enough. To know what you are talking about requires not only self-knowledge but also knowledge of the world outside. Facts and figures are not to be dismissed as the property of pedants, academicians, and squares. You need to have information to make good sense, and your job is to find information. Then, to influence an audience to believe in the rightness of your position and to have a significant influence, you must present your material interestingly, colorfully, and beautifully. You must give your audience something of yourself.

Think about yourself. Whom do you listen to? Don't you respond more easily to beautiful words and effective speaking? Beautiful speech doen't mean flowery language, of course: it means concise, precise, and exact expression. If you know something, you can say it. Don't rely upon that cliché which lies, 'I know what I want to say, but I don't know how to say it." If you know what you have to say, you can find the words.

I have asked you in this book to do several kinds of formal speaking, to participate in a discussion or debate, to make a persuasive speech, to interpret prose and poetry, to act. In your lifetime, you may never be called upon to do any of these things in a formal way. But you will do all of them in an informal way so that you may be heard and seen.

Your job is just beginning. Getting to know yourself and the persons to whom you speak is a full-time task. I think it is a worthwhile task, and if you remember this book, it will be when you find genuine pleasure and excitement in talking to other people. People do indeed need people, and part of that need is fulfilled by talking to one another. There is no limit to this. We never run out of talk. And, as far as this book is concerned, in the end is the beginning.

So it goes.